LIVE
BIG
LOVE
BIGGER

RECLAIMING YOUR LIFE
ONE MOMENT AT A TIME

LIVE
BIG
LOVE
BIGGER

DR. KHARA BETH SKIDGEL

First Edition
ISBN: 979-8-89898-770-1
Printed in the United States of America

Cover Design by: Dr. Khara Beth Skidgel
Interior Design and Layout by: Dr. Khara Beth Skidgel

Author Disclaimer

This book is a work of nonfiction based on the author's personal experiences, reflections, and opinions. Some names, identifying characteristics, and events have been changed, condensed, or combined for the sake of privacy, storytelling flow, and confidentiality.

The author has made every effort to protect the identities of individuals and to portray events as truthfully and compassionately as possible from her perspective. Any resemblance to real persons, living or dead, beyond those explicitly acknowledged, is purely coincidental.

This book is not intended to defame, malign, or harm any individual, group, or organization. The views expressed are those of the author and are not intended as statements of absolute fact. The author disclaims any liability for any perceived harm, injury, or loss incurred as a result of reading this book.

This content is for inspirational and informational purposes only. It is not a substitute for professional advice, including but not limited to legal, therapeutic, medical, or spiritual counsel.

Table of Contents

To every woman who's ever felt invisible,
broken, silenced, or small—
this is for you.

To the ones who kept going with tired hearts, who whispered
prayers through tears,
who chose to rise again when no one was watching—
you are not alone.

This book is a love letter
to the girl I once was,
to the mother I had to become,
and to the warrior I found along the way.

May these pages remind you
that healing is not linear,
bravery is not loud,
and you can reclaim your life
one brave, sacred, ordinary moment at a time.

Live big.
Love bigger.
You were made for this.

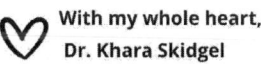 With my whole heart,
Dr. Khara Skidgel

Introduction

The Power of a Moment

"She gave this name to the Lord who spoke to her: 'You are the God who sees me.'" —Genesis 16:13

I didn't count days like other people.

I didn't count holidays, or milestones, or anniversaries. I counted survival.

I counted moments.

There was a notebook. Just a simple spiral-bound pad that I kept in my bathroom makeup drawer. Inside, it wasn't filled with words or poetry or plans. It was filled with symbols. Circles. Numbers. Slashes. Marks that only I understood.

Each number meant a day. Each day meant I'd made it.

That I had survived.

A circle? That meant the abuse happened in the morning.

A filled-in circle? It happened again at night.

A slash? It was physical.

Some pages looked like artwork—a cruel kind of abstract design, shaped by trauma, shaded by fear. I used to stare at those pages, hoping someone would notice the pattern and ask. No one ever did. But I kept counting.

Somewhere along the line, I stopped believing that healing could be big or beautiful. I believed it had to be tiny, hidden. I believed if I could just string together enough bearable moments, then maybe—just maybe—I could breathe. Maybe I could stay. Maybe I could survive.

I had learned—over time and through trauma—that attention came at a cost. If I stood too tall, spoke too freely, cried too loudly, or dared to dream too publicly, something would snap. I had been conditioned to believe that safety lived in the shadows. So, I kept my pain polite and my hope microscopic. I didn't dare ask for transformation. I asked for tolerance. I didn't believe I could be made whole—I just begged not to fall apart completely.

It wasn't just fear. It was shame. A shame that clung to me like a second skin, whispering lies in the dark: You stayed too long. You knew better. You let it happen. I thought I had forfeited the right to big healing. I thought God might still love me—but only in quiet ways. Only from a distance. So, I scaled my healing down to something I could hide. Something no one else had to see. Something small enough to tuck between mascara tubes and broken bobby pins in my bathroom drawer.

I believed if I could just string together enough bearable moments, then maybe—just maybe—I could breathe. Maybe I could stay. Maybe I could survive. And maybe that would be enough.

But this book?

This book is not about surviving.

This book is about what happens when you stop counting moments of survival and start claiming moments of courage.

This book is about the shift. The sacred, excruciating, holy shift when you realize you don't have to live afraid. That you don't have to disappear to stay safe. That you can live big. And love bigger. And rebuild the life you were always worthy of.

I wrote this book because there was a version of me who needed to read it—but couldn't find it. A version of me who was so buried under shame, silence, and self-doubt that I thought maybe brokenness was just where I was meant to live. A version of me who believed in everyone's redemption story but her own.

She wasn't flashy or loud or brave on the outside. She was tired. Hollow-eyed. Her smile had started to curl at the edges like old paper. She wore sweatshirts and extra makeup to hide the bruises on her body—and the ones no one could see. She tiptoed through her own home like an uninvited guest, shrinking her voice to keep the peace, rationing her laughter like it might cost too much.

I remember her standing in front of the mirror at 3 a.m.—hands trembling, mascara smudged, eyes searching for a trace of the girl she used to be. She was staring at someone she didn't recognize but was too scared to leave behind. She whispered, this can't be it... right? But she didn't believe she deserved anything more.

She was buried under shame so thick it felt like cement. Silenced by fear. Paralyzed by the belief that she had missed her chance at a different life. She believed in everyone else's healing. Everyone else's happy ending. Everyone else's freedom. Just not her own.

This book is for her.

And if that's where you are?

You are not alone.

If you've ever stayed too long in a relationship that hurt you... If you've ever made yourself smaller just to keep someone else comfortable... If you've ever been told that you're too much, or not enough... If you've ever wept on the bathroom floor and whispered, "God, where are You?"...

Then this book is for you.

Not because I have all the answers. I don't. I still wrestle. I still question. But I finally stopped lying about the questions. I stopped pretending they didn't keep me up at night. I stopped numbing them, silencing them, stuffing them behind polite smiles and perfectly worded prayers. I let them rise. I let them breathe. I let them lead me back to the God who can handle all of it—every doubt, every ache, every tear-soaked why.

And here's what I found:

Healing is not a finish line. Healing is a rhythm. A choice. A sacred daily turning.

It's not loud or dramatic. Most days it's quiet and stubborn—barely noticeable to the outside world. It looks like standing up when everything in you wants to crawl back into bed. It looks like whispering a promise over your own heart—I am safe now. I am loved. I am healing. It looks like lighting a candle in the dark just to remind yourself the darkness doesn't win. It looks like taking a deep breath and choosing not to text the person who hurt you. Again.

Healing is returning—again and again—to the truth of who you are and whose you are.

The kind of turning that happens in real time, in real mess, in real faith. The kind that happens one brave moment at a time.

I named this book Live Big Love Bigger because those four words are what pulled me out of the dark.

They were the whisper in my spirit when I was too afraid to speak. They were the nudge when I wanted to go back. They were the compass when I didn't know what came next.

To live big doesn't mean to live loud. It means to live honest. Whole. Unhidden. Unashamed. To love bigger doesn't mean to love others more than yourself. It means to include yourself in the love you give so freely.

This book is built in moments—sacred, messy, ordinary moments that led me out of fear and into freedom. Each chapter tells part of my story. Not polished. Not perfect. Just real.

Every chapter, you'll also find a challenge:

- A Live It Out Challenge: an invitation to act bravely in your own life, or,
- A Love Bigger Challenge: a reminder that loving well starts with grace for yourself.

You don't have to do it all at once.

You don't have to fix everything to begin healing.

You just have to take the next brave step.

In my deepest pain, I learned this:

The breaking point is sacred.

Not polished. Not pretty. But holy.

It didn't feel holy when it happened. It felt like collapse.

I remember the moment. The exact breath. The way the air tasted—like dust and disbelief. I was on the floor of my bathroom, knees pressed into cold tile, heart racing so loudly I could barely hear my own cries. There was no dramatic goodbye. No swelling music. Just silence. The kind that fills a room when the last piece of your pretending finally gives out.

It wasn't loud. It was quieter than I expected—like a building falling inward. No one heard it but me.

And in that silence, I broke.

I wept. Not gentle tears—gut-wrenching, snot-dripping, grief-born sobs. I wept for the years I lost. I wept for the girl I abandoned to keep someone else whole. I wept because I didn't know how to go forward—but I couldn't go back.

But before I could name what was happening in me, I kept thinking of a woman from the Bible who had been cast out too.

Her name was Hagar.

She didn't ask for the suffering that came into her life. She was used. Dismissed. Sent away into the desert with nothing but a skin of water and a child in her arms. She didn't have a support system or a safety plan. She didn't even have a voice in her own story—at least not at first.

And when everything collapsed, Hagar did what so many of us do.

She broke.

She laid her child under a bush and walked away because she couldn't bear to watch him die. She wept alone, believing she had been abandoned. Forgotten.

But she wasn't.

God met her there—in the middle of the wilderness. He didn't scold her. He didn't shame her. He called her by name.

And for the first time in Scripture, someone gives God a name:

El Roi. "The God who sees me."

That story has followed me. Because there was a version of me that, like Hagar, thought maybe God had stopped looking.

That maybe I had disqualified myself from His closeness.

That maybe all He had for me was silence.

But like Hagar, I discovered something in my wilderness.

God hadn't stopped seeing me.

I had just stopped believing I was worth looking at.

Like Hagar weeping in the wilderness, I had run far from what broke me—but didn't know where to go. I wasn't sure if God would show up in the dry places. I didn't know if He saw me anymore. But in the middle of my nothingness, I heard a whisper deep in my spirit—not loud, not forced, just steady and sure: I see you. I know your name.

And that changed everything.

Because when God speaks your name in the wilderness, it becomes a place of promise. When He sees you in your breaking, you realize the breaking isn't the end—it's the beginning of something brand new.

You may not know how to rebuild yet. You may not see the future clearly.

But if you're still breathing, God is still moving. You are still becoming.

So, take a deep breath. Put your hand over your heart. And remember: You're not behind. You're not broken beyond repair. You're just standing in your moment.

Welcome to the beginning. Welcome to Live Big Love Bigger

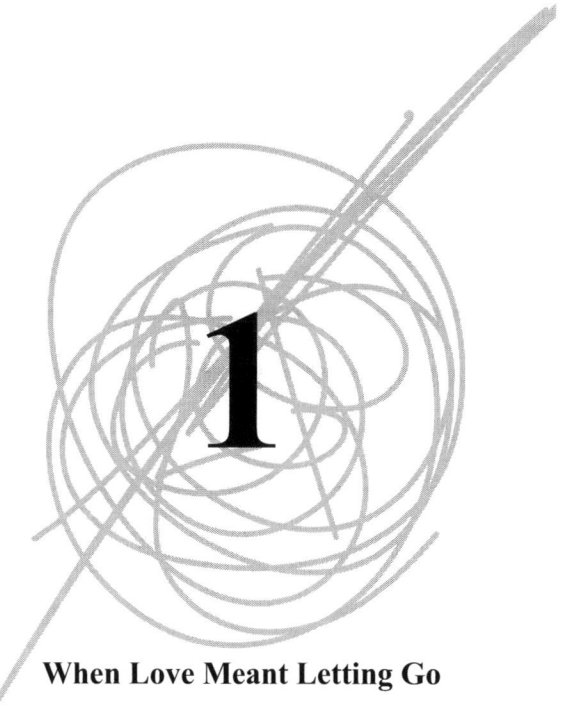

When Love Meant Letting Go

"The Lord is close to the brokenhearted and saves those who are crushed in spirit." —Psalm 34:18

The door didn't slam behind me. That's what most people assume. But it wasn't that kind of moment. There was no shouting. No grand declaration of freedom. No dramatic exit.

Just silence.

A kind of silence that presses against your chest, tightening like a vice. The kind that comes after years of keeping things inside. After crying quietly in the shower so no one could hear. After making excuses and hiding bruises—on your skin and in your soul.

The kind of silence that screams without sound: Everything has changed.
That night started with a text message. Fourteen words. Fourteen words
that told us to leave our home—again. For what felt like the hundredth
time. Only this time felt different. Heavy.

Because this time, it didn't just feel cruel. It felt final.

We had been together for six years. Long enough to build a life. Long
enough to forget where one chapter ended and the next began. Long
enough for our children to consider themselves siblings. We blended
birthdays and Christmas mornings. We built routines and expanded our
company. We built a home, blessed it and dreamt of the future.

Our home. We had poured everything into that place.

We trenched water lines. Hauled off rusted metal scraps. Roofed barns in
scorching heat. Dug up stubborn yucca plants whose roots ran deeper
than our patience. Every square inch of that land held sweat and
memories.

We built each room with love. We hand-picked every knob, the paint
colors, and piece of trim. We design custom-built ins just for us. Argued
over how big to make the kitchen island and which mirrors to buy. That
island was a compromise, a symbol of the family we were trying to be.

It wasn't just a house.

It was our life.

And in one text—one moment—we were told to walk away from all of it.
That 14-word text told me to leave–but my soul had already started
walking toward the door. I had spent too long pretending. Pretending it
wasn't that bad. Pretending it was just stress. Pretending that love was
supposed to hurt.

So many other times, I would have begged to stay.

I would have pleaded for understanding, twisted my words into apologies, and tried—once again—to explain things that should have never needed an explanation.

Like why we celebrated my son's birthday the way we did. Why I let him laugh too loudly, or invited too many people, or smiled too much when he opened his gift. In a healthy relationship, that would've been a moment of joy. But in mine, it became a trigger. A perceived offense. Something I was expected to justify, tone down, or redo to make someone else more comfortable.

Or why the boys went to see their biological dad in the hospital. He was experiencing heart failure, and they needed to see him—to understand, to connect, to process. But even that became a source of tension. I was expected to defend their presence there. I was accused of betrayal, of disloyalty, for allowing them to show empathy to the man who gave them life.

These were moments that should have been simple. Human. Compassionate. Celebrating a child's life. Visiting a sick parent. But in an abusive relationship, normal becomes complicated. Kindness requires permission. And your instincts get twisted so tightly that you begin to question yourself for doing the most loving thing.

I lived in that tension for too long—constantly managing someone else's emotions while suppressing my own. Constantly explaining my decisions, my tone, my motives, my heart.

And each time, I sacrificed a piece of myself in the name of peace.

But that night, I didn't do it.

I didn't explain. I didn't defend. I didn't try to earn the right to stay.

Because somewhere deep down, I finally realized: I didn't need permission to be kind. I didn't need to justify being a good mother. I didn't need to beg for safety or convince anyone that my children's joy, grief, or healing was valid.

I just needed to leave.

That night, the boys helped me load the car. It was quiet work. I didn't even have to ask them. They just... knew. That still wrecks me. Because they shouldn't have had to know.

I watched my boys carry a laundry basket filled with clothes and our backpacks to the trunk. No tears. No questions. Just calm. My oldest son looked at me like he saw something I hadn't yet noticed: the beginning. But I couldn't see it—not yet.

All I saw was the end.

I remember staring at the house one last time, watching the porch lights dim as I drove down the winding road. Not because it was home—but because it represented everything I had tried to hold together. The image. The safety. The lie.

As I passed the gate one last time, unglued and unraveling, I felt the layers of a life I had crafted with sheer determination begin to fall away. My hands trembled. My breath was shallow. My knees were weak.

I wasn't just leaving a place. I was leaving a version of myself behind. The one who had mastered survival. The one who shrank to fit. The one who believed that silence was strength.

And in those last seconds, something inside me broke. And something else awakened.

Because underneath all the fear and chaos... was the tiniest flicker of peace.

That flicker was God. Not in the lightning. Not in the fire. In the whisper.

People ask what a "breaking point" feels like.

It feels like staring at the rearview mirror with tears you don't have time to cry. It feels like hearing your son ask, "Are we going to be okay?"—and not knowing the answer.

That night, I felt like a modern-day Hagar in the wilderness—cast out, used up, holding my child with no clear direction, no water left, and nothing but empty sky above me.

Like her, I laid everything down—my hope, my strength, my pride—and waited in the silence. I didn't know where help would come from. I just knew I couldn't stay in the place that broke me.

And just like Hagar, God met me there. Not with a rescue plan. Not with a roadmap. But with presence.

A whisper in the wreckage: "I see you."

It feels like holding a steering wheel with one hand and holding your heart together with the other.

It feels like guilt. Relief. Grief. Freedom. All tangled together.

But there's this one moment—this one second—that I'll never forget.

My son put his hand on my shoulder. I hadn't even realized I was shaking. He looked at me and said, "We've got each other, Mom. That's enough."

I broke.

Not because I was weak—but because those words reached a place inside me, I'd long buried.

And I knew, deep in my bones, that this wasn't just a breakdown. It was a breakthrough.

It's strange how clarity often comes wrapped in chaos.

That night, everything was uncertain. We didn't know what it would feel like. We didn't know what the next day would bring. We didn't know if we would ever get our things back or finality of the moment.

But I knew—absolutely knew—we couldn't stay.

Staying would've kept me silent. Staying would've told my sons that abuse was something you tolerate. Staying would've taught them that love hurts and truth hides.

Leaving hurt. But staying would've killed something deeper. Because here's the truth that no one talks about: when you stay too long in a place that breaks you, you start to steal from yourself.

You steal your own joy.

You rob yourself of peace.

You trade your voice for temporary comfort.

You teach yourself that worthiness is negotiable.

And worst of all?

You start to believe the lie that you can endure anything—even if it costs you everything.

You begin to adapt to the ache.

You decorate the damage.

You normalize the numb.

But you weren't created to just survive brokenness. You were created to rise from it.

And here's what I learned: you don't have to keep fighting every battle yourself.

There comes a moment where you stop swinging and start surrendering.

When you stop exhausting yourself trying to fix what was never yours to carry.

Because in trauma, the enemy doesn't just attack your situation—he attacks your soul.

He comes for your passion. He tries to dim your spirit. He steals your desire for prayer. He manipulates your perspective and magnifies your insecurities.

And slowly, your soul house begins to collapse.

Just like Hagar sat down across from her child, believing they would die in the desert, I felt that soul-deep ache—when you think the story ends here.

But the same God who opened Hagar's eyes to a hidden well opened my spirit to a flicker of peace. Not a flood. Not a roar. Just a flicker.

And that flicker was enough to remind me: I was seen. And I was not done.

Imagine it—each moment of abuse I had marked in that notepad was like a new room being destroyed.

Each number another piece of my peace torn down. Each circle another corner of my spirit left littered, hollowed out, abandoned.

Until all that's left is rubble where a sanctuary once stood.

But here's the truth: God rebuilds.

The enemy may destroy, but God restores. And you don't have to defend every door of that house alone. The Lord will fight for you; you need only to be still. (Exodus 14:14)

I used to keep track of every moment of pain. I thought if I could just count enough days, enough mornings, enough nights—if I could organize the trauma, I could control it.

But that notebook—that heartbreaking, coded record of my abuse—had no place anymore. Because we were leaving the house. And I was leaving that part of me. That notebook didn't get packed. It didn't come with us.

Because that version of me, the one who chronicled every hurt as if survival depended on it, was done. She was tired. And she was finally allowed to rest.

We parked in front of my parents' house late that evening. It was quiet. Safe. No one asked questions. No one judged. They just opened the door. I watched my boys walk in the front door; their faces relaxed for the first time in what felt like years.

And I wept. Not loud. Not messy. Just long, silent tears that carried years of pain out through my skin.

I looked up at the stars that night and whispered, "God, I don't know what I'm doing. But please... don't leave us now."

And I felt it.

Not a voice. Not a sign.

Just presence.

Like God was sitting with me, holding space for my grief.

Psalm 34:18 came to mind: "The Lord is close to the brokenhearted and saves those who are crushed in spirit."

That verse wasn't abstract anymore.

It was the air I breathed.

I used to think strength was about holding it all together.

Now I know real strength is the moment you finally let go.

Letting go of shame.

Letting go of pretending.

Letting go of needing permission to choose yourself.

That night wasn't clean or pretty. I didn't have a "plan." I didn't have a savings account or next steps lined up.

What I had was truth. And my children. And that was enough to begin.

You never forget your breaking point. But you also never forget who stood with you in it.

My sons weren't just witnesses to my pain. They were quiet warriors beside me. They saw the truth before I could. They didn't push me—they simply stood with me until I was ready.

That's what love looks like in its purest form.

And now, every time I think about that moment, I don't just remember the ache—I remember the shift.

The sacred shift from I can't to maybe I can.

From this is the end to what if this is just the beginning?

I used to be ashamed of that night.

Ashamed that I had no plan. Ashamed that I stayed as long as I did.

Ashamed that my kids had to see me unravel.

But now?

That night is holy ground. Because it's where I stopped hiding. It's where I realized that rock bottom isn't a curse—it's a foundation. And on that foundation, I would slowly begin to rebuild.

Not overnight.

Not without setbacks.

But brick by brick—with truth, with grace, and with the kind of love that comes from being fully seen.

If you're reading this and you're at your breaking point, I want you to hear this:

You're not crazy. You're not weak. You're not failing.

You are rising.

Maybe you, too, feel cast aside. Maybe you've been told your story doesn't matter. Maybe you're surviving a wilderness no one else can see. Let Hagar remind you: God sees you. He meets women in the desert. He calls them by name. He turns breaking points into wells of living water. And He's doing that for you, even now.

Even if your legs are trembling under the weight of it all.

Even if your voice is barely a whisper.

Even if you feel like you're crawling more than standing—you are still rising.

Even if you don't feel it yet.

Even if you don't know what comes next.

Even if every breath feels like a battle, you are not losing. You are living. God is close. Closer than your next breath. Closer than the tear that hasn't yet fallen. Your pain is real, but it will not be permanent.

You may not be able to change the past—but you have full authority to choose the next brave moment.

And sometimes, that's where the miracle begins.

Not in the fixing. Not in the planning.

But in the choosing. In the showing up. In the opening of your heart again.

Because here's the power that trauma doesn't want you to find you can reframe the moment.

You can choose to stop carrying the lies that were never yours to begin with. You can take that memory—that moment where everything felt like it shattered—and speak new truth into it. You can say: this isn't where I end. This is where I begin.

When you start telling the truth—your truth—the atmosphere shifts. The enemy loses his grip. The shame loses its sting. And you begin to hear a new narrative rise up in your spirit:

"I am not what happened to me. I am what I choose to become."

Your voice is powerful. It may have been silenced, but it was never destroyed. You get to speak life over your story. You get to rise with power, with clarity, with holy defiance.

Because no one—no abuser, no fear, no past—can take away what God placed inside you.

You get to live on purpose. You get to build again. And every time you speak truth over your wounds, you lay a new brick in the house of your healing.

So, when the voices come—the ones that say you should've left sooner, or stayed longer, or done it differently—you tell them this:

"I am not defined by delay. I am defined by the decision I made to move forward."

You don't have to be fully healed to be holy.

You don't have to be fearless to be faithful.

You just have to take the next step.

That moment—that one brave, trembling, holy moment—can start right now. And it counts more than you know.

"Then the King will say to those on his right, 'Come, you who are blessed by my Father; take your inheritance, the kingdom prepared for you since the creation of the world.'" —Matthew 25:34

Live It Out Challenge | Honor Your Breaking Point

There's a holy kind of strength in naming the place where it all fell apart. Not to stay there. Not to relive the pain. But to recognize it for what it truly was: the moment courage began to stir.

Just like Hagar in the wilderness—tired, used, unseen—you may have reached a point where you thought the story was over. But that moment, that breaking point, wasn't abandonment. It was invitation.

An invitation to be seen. To start again. To walk toward freedom.

God met Hagar in her most broken place. Not with blame. Not with judgment. But with a question: "Where have you come from, and where are you going?" (Genesis 16:8)

Let Him meet you now.

Reflect & Write

Take a few quiet moments today—not to reopen wounds, but to honor the moment your soul started whispering, "There's more than this."

Turn to the Heart Notes section in the back of this book and write with honesty and tenderness. Don't edit. Don't filter. Just tell your truth.

Ask yourself:

- What did I leave behind that day?

  (A lie I believed? A version of myself I outgrew?)

- What did I begin to reclaim, even if I didn't know it yet?

  (Peace? Voice? The right to dream again?)

- Who stood with me when I couldn't stand on my own?

  (A child. A parent. A friend. God.)

Then—like Hagar—mark this moment. Name it.

Write this truth somewhere you'll see it often: on your bathroom mirror, on a sticky note in your planner, or whispered each morning into your breath:

"My breaking point is not my weakness. It was my beginning."

"For when I am weak, then I am strong." —2 Corinthians 12:10

Anchor Prayer | The God Who Sees Me

God who sees me,

When the silence stretches long

and I wonder if anyone notices—

You do.

You saw me when I couldn't lift my eyes.

You found me in the wilderness.

You called me by name.

When the weight of shame tells me I'm too late,

too lost,

too damaged to be loved—

You whisper,

"You are not too broken to begin again."

You anoint my becoming, even here.

Especially here.

So, I return to the well—

not just to drink,

but to remember.

You are the God who saw Hagar.

You are the God who sees me.

And even when I feel invisible to the world,

I am held in full view of heaven.

I am not behind. I am not unseen. I am not abandoned.

I am becoming.

And becoming is holy ground.

Let this truth find root in my dry places.

Let it become my rhythm of return—

my quiet courage, my brave beginning, my sacred yes.

Amen.

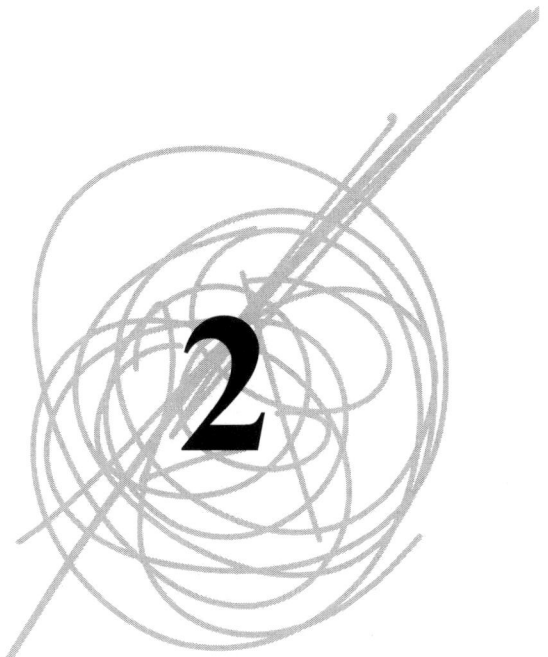

2

Becoming the Woman I Didn't Yet Believe In

"She is clothed with strength and dignity; she can laugh at the days to come." —Proverbs 31:25

We quote that verse so easily, don't we? We print it on mugs, journals, wall art. But the woman in Proverbs 31 isn't a slogan—she's a blueprint. Not of perfection, but of purpose.

She is strong—not because she hasn't known sorrow, but because she's chosen resilience.

She's dignified—not because of a perfect past, but because she knows where her worth comes from.

She plans, she builds, she nurtures, she speaks wisdom, and she guards her home with boldness.

She's not afraid of the future—not because she has it all figured out, but because she knows who holds it.

This woman doesn't arrive polished and perfect. She becomes—over time, in layers, through ordinary choices, holy confidence, and sacred obedience. And when I was staring into a foggy mirror, searching for a glimpse of the woman I hoped I could become… she gave me a vision. Not to compare myself. But to believe in who I could become through grace.

But grace doesn't transform you in an instant—it invites you into a process.

I didn't wake up the next morning walking in holy confidence or laughing at the future. I woke up groggy, grieving, and unsure of what came next. I had a glimpse of who I could become, but I hadn't stepped into her shoes yet. I was still barefoot in the hallway, staring at laundry baskets filled with pieces of my life. And that's when I learned: becoming her—the woman of strength and dignity—starts not with big declarations, but with small decisions.

Healing doesn't come with a welcome mat. It doesn't burst through the door with clarity and closure. It comes quietly—on the heels of silence, woven through ordinary moments that feel too small to matter. And those are the hardest days—the ones no one prepares you for. You think healing will feel rewarding, loud, maybe even cinematic. Like a confetti moment where you suddenly realize the pain is over and your strength has arrived. But that's not how it works.

Healing shows up in the mundane. It's brushing your teeth through tears. It's folding laundry with a knot in your stomach. It's answering texts when all you want is to disappear. Healing asks you to keep showing up even when your soul begs to hide. The world around you looks the same while everything inside you is screaming for change. The ordinary becomes heavy. The silence stretches on. But it's in that place—beneath the weight of the unseen—where real strength is born. Not in the spotlight. In the shadows. In the private yeses no one sees. In the moments where you choose life even when it doesn't feel like it's choosing you.

I woke up the morning after we were kicked out of our home in the bedroom I grew up in, wrapped in blankets that weren't mine, in a house that no longer felt like home. The walls were familiar, but I wasn't. The girl who once dreamed behind those four walls had become a woman I barely recognized. A mother. A fighter. A soul trying to breathe. My body was there, but my spirit was still curled in a tight ball somewhere deep inside me. I remember thinking, I want to go home. And then the ache that followed: Where is home now?

That first morning, I couldn't move. My legs felt like stone. My heart like glass. And yet, somehow, my son walked in—sleepy-eyed and gentle— and asked, "What's for breakfast?" That's the thing about trauma: it doesn't pause for real life. It meets you in it. It doesn't wait for the right time. It crashes into routines and wrecks your sense of safety. It turns simple tasks into mountains. It steals your joy and replaces it with dread. It convinces you that pain is normal, deserved, or inescapable. If you let it, trauma will set up residence in the very soul house God designed for peace and purpose.

But something holy happens when you start naming it. Truthfully. Tenderly. Boldly.

So, I made eggs. I poured cereal. I brushed my hair. Every one of those tiny acts became sacred. They weren't just chores. They were declarations. I am still here. Even if I don't know who I'm becoming yet. The unraveling hadn't begun that night. It began much earlier, in quieter ways that are easy to overlook. Abuse doesn't always show up as bruises. Sometimes, it begins with shredded cheese.

We were only a few weeks into dating. I remember making tacos, and I grabbed some shredded cheese and got a piece on the counter by accident. I remember the moment so vividly—not because of what was said, but how it made me feel. The rage in his eyes. The sharp tone in his voice "You're just going to leave that there? You really are as useless as you look." before I knew it the plate was snatched from my hands and was tossed across the room in disgust.

It wasn't the volume. It was the violence in his energy. The belittling. The shift. I froze. And then I apologized. I told myself he was tired, that I needed to be more careful. But deep down, something inside me knew this wasn't okay. That moment—so small on the outside—was the first time I forgot my worth to keep the peace. And that forgetting snowballed into years of shrinking.

The enemy thrives in the space between breaking and becoming. He whispers: "You left, but what now?" "You think you're strong but look at you." "You're nothing without him." He magnifies our insecurities and distorts our reflection until we can no longer see the Proverbs 31 woman in the mirror. Instead, we see our failures. Our stretch marks. Our shame. We downplay our strengths. We highlight our flaws. We shrink to fit the image someone else gave us. And slowly, we forget who we are.

But God doesn't.

The Proverbs 31 woman is not a Pinterest-perfect ideal. She is not praised for her beauty, but for her fear of the Lord. She is clothed with strength and dignity. She makes bold decisions. She cares for her family and extends her hands to the poor. She laughs without fear of the future—not because she knows what's coming, but because she knows who holds it. She is not fragile. She is fierce. And when I forgot who I was, she was the woman I had to remember—not perfect, but powerful. Not flawless, but faithful.

But long before I could even see glimpses of the Proverbs 31 woman in myself, I had to meet someone else—someone who felt more like me in the messy middle.

Her name was Leah.

You might know her as the "unloved wife," the one Jacob didn't choose. Her story is often overshadowed by her sister Rachel, who had the beauty, the favor, the love Leah never got. Leah was married through deceit, used as a pawn, and left aching in a marriage where she constantly had to earn affection.

But here's what wrecked me:

God saw her.

In Genesis 29, scripture says "When the Lord saw that Leah was not loved, he enabled her to conceive…" (v.31). Every time she bore a child, she named them with a cry of longing: Maybe now my husband will love me.

Maybe now I'll be enough.

Maybe now I'll be seen.

Leah was a woman becoming—but didn't yet believe in herself.

And I get that.

Because like Leah, I spent years trying to be chosen. I twisted myself into the version I thought someone else would love. I measured my worth by how wanted I felt. And when that love didn't come—or came with conditions—I told myself I just needed to work harder, get smaller, love better.

But then something shifted in Leah.

When she birthed her fourth son, Judah, she said: "This time I will praise the Lord."

Not "maybe now I'll be loved."

Not "maybe now I'll be enough."

Just praise.

It was her turning point.

And it became mine.

Leah today might be the woman scrolling social media, comparing her life to curated snapshots of someone else's highlight reel. She's the woman who bends and breaks to be loved—believing she has to earn what should be freely given. She's the woman doing all the "right" things but feeling invisible in her own home, her own heart. She wears her resilience like armor but secretly wonders if she's actually worthy of joy. She is becoming.

But she doesn't believe it yet.

And just like God saw Leah in the shadows of rejection, He sees you too—in the stretch marks, in the sacrifice, in the morning breath and the late-night tears. You don't have to become perfect to be praised. You just have to be present.

In the stillness of that first morning, something subtle stirred. It wasn't dramatic. It didn't announce itself. But it was there—a whisper, like breath in lungs held too long. The light through the curtains reminded me of childhood. The air smelled familiar. I felt grounded, not because I had answers, but because I sensed I was no longer lost. That stillness wasn't empty. It was sacred. It was the beginning of something I couldn't name yet but desperately needed.

I remember sitting in the driver's seat the night we left, hands gripping the wheel like it was the only thing tethering me to earth. The car was still. My sons were silent in the backseat. The air felt thick, like time had frozen. I had just heard the words that fractured everything: "I'm done. You better not be there when I get home. Don't come back." I couldn't breathe. I couldn't move. Until my son said gently, "Mom… it's time to leave."

That sentence shattered the fog. It reminded me I wasn't alone. It reminded me I was still a mother, still worthy, still seen. That second— the moment I felt supported—was the crack in the foundation where light first entered.

Back at my parents' house, reality came crashing in. We weren't just emotionally wrecked. We were physically displaced. Every sock, every toothbrush, every school form was stuffed into laundry baskets and bags lining their hallway. We had no roadmap. Just silence, heartbreak, and a fragile hope that God was still writing our story.

Starting over with nothing strips you to your bones. It humbles you. It makes you question everything you thought you knew. But God doesn't need polished plans. He needs surrendered hearts. And mine—though broken—was wide open.

So, I ran. Miles and miles. Some days, like I was chasing healing. Other days, like I was running from the weight of it all. I kept pushing through my doctorate, even when the words on the screen blurred through exhausted tears. I journaled one sentence a day: God, help me. On the brave days: God, thank You for not letting go. I folded laundry to Maverick City. I stared at scripture until I could say it out loud again— half whisper, half war cry.

I stopped counting moments of pain. I started marking moments of peace. The journal that once documented trauma became a record of survival. I wasn't just keeping track of time. I was testifying to life.

And the woman I was becoming? She didn't look like victory. She wore a messy bun. She reheated her coffee three times and still didn't finish it. She cried into towels. She whispered scripture with trembling lips. But she was there. Stubborn. Present. Brave in ways only heaven saw.

I couldn't see her clearly yet. But she was rising.

Healing doesn't restore what was broken—it makes it holy.

You don't rebuild your life all at once. You heal in layers. You reclaim your voice in whispers before roars. You get dressed in strength one sleeve at a time. And eventually, you begin to believe I am not too much. I am not too late. You see your reflection as holy ground again.

I am the woman who left. The woman who stayed gone. The woman who kept choosing healing, even when it didn't feel brave. And so are you.

If you're somewhere between broken and becoming—keep going.

The woman you don't yet believe in is real. And she's waiting on the other side of today's yes.

Love Bigger Challenge | Rediscover Your Reflection

You are not defined by who you were in survival mode.

You are becoming.

When you've spent years shrinking, it's hard to see yourself clearly. The mirror often reflects what pain taught you to believe: too loud. Too quiet. Too much. Not enough.

But that reflection isn't your enemy—it's your invitation.

> To stand still.

> To stop apologizing.

> To start seeing the woman God is forming

Soul Work:

Find a mirror—any mirror. Your bathroom, your car visor, your rearview.

Stand there. One full minute. No adjusting. No looking away. No apologies.

Let your eyes settle on the woman in front of you.

Then speak this truth out loud—even if your voice shakes:

> "I am clothed in strength and dignity. I am not who I was. I am who God is making me to be."
>
> —Proverbs 31:25

Now, take a sticky note or small card. Write a blessing or promise to your reflection—just one line: something you need to hear, something your soul is still learning to believe. Tape it to the mirror. Leave it there.

Let it be a daily declaration that loving bigger starts with how you see yourself.

Anchor Prayer | The Mirror and the Maker

Heavenly Father,

Some days I avoid the mirror.

Not because I don't care—but because I'm afraid of what I'll see.

I've carried labels that weren't mine.

I've absorbed lies whispered by fear,

rejection, comparison, and pain.

But You see me differently.

Not through the lens of shame, but through the lens of becoming.

Today, help me see what You see.

Not just skin and scars, but the strength stitched into my spirit.

The dignity that never left me.

The beauty of a soul that chose to stay—

to heal, to rise, to return.

Quiet the voices that tell me I'm not enough.

Remind me that I am Your masterpiece—

not finished but already loved.

Let my reflection become holy ground.

Let it testify not to my flaws—but to my fight.

And when I forget again—because I will—

draw me back to this moment.

Back to the mirror. Back to Your eyes.

Back to the truth:

I am clothed in strength and dignity. I am not who I was.

I am who You are making me to be.

Amen.

3

Reclaiming Truth

"Then you will know the truth, and the truth will set you free."

—John 8:32

For years, I thought maybe it really was me.

That I was too emotional. Too dramatic. Too sensitive. Too loud. Too soft. Too… something. I couldn't name it exactly, but I lived in a constant state of walking on eggshells—carefully shaping myself into whatever version of me wouldn't set him off.

That's what gaslighting does. It doesn't just distort the truth. It disorients you. You stop trusting your instincts. You lose the ability to stand on solid ground because the rules keep changing. You start to believe that

25

your memory is flawed, your feelings are exaggerated, and your pain is proof of your own failure.

He didn't need to call me crazy. He didn't have to. The way conversations were twisted, denied things clearly said, or responded with "you always do this" or "I never said that" was enough to do the job. Over time, I stopped reacting. Not because I didn't feel it—but because I no longer knew if I had the right to.

The manipulation wasn't always loud. It was often so subtle I couldn't explain it to anyone else—just quiet contradictions that left me unraveling at the seams.

There were moments I'd stand in the kitchen trying to remember why I felt upset, and all I could find was a knot in my stomach and the dull ache of being emotionally erased. Things I knew had happened were suddenly rewritten. Conversations disappeared, motives were questioned, and any pain I expressed was thrown back at me as "proof" of my instability.

I began keeping journals—not to process, but to remember. To anchor myself to something tangible when my reality was constantly being questioned. I saved screenshots of texts, wrote down exact phrases, not for revenge, but survival. I needed to know I wasn't imagining it.

And yet—I still questioned everything.

There's one night I'll never forget. Not because it was explosive, but because it was just… familiar. The same pattern, the same script. It started with something small. It always did. This time, a comment about how long I'd been in the shower. The implication was clear—I was being selfish. Hiding. Avoiding him. Within minutes, it spiraled. The accusations, the yelling, the slamming of doors. And my heart, pounding in my chest like a drum I couldn't quiet.

I locked myself in the bathroom. The tile was cold beneath my legs. I pulled one of the boys' old towels from the hook to muffle my sobs—not because I was ashamed, but because I knew if he heard me, it would be worse.

I remember thinking, this can't be normal.

I wasn't crying because of what he said. I was crying because I was tired of crying about the same things. Over. And over. And over again.

In those minutes, something unexpected happened.

I started choosing.

Not loudly. Not bravely in the way we talk about bravery. But quietly. Subtly. I chose not to engage. I chose silence. I chose not to defend myself to someone who wasn't really listening. I chose to send a text to a friend and simply say: "I'm not okay."

I chose to pray, even if I wasn't sure anyone was listening. I stared at the ceiling and noticed a crack that looked like a lightning bolt. For some reason, that tiny fracture steadied me.

Maybe that's what I am now, I thought. Cracked. But still here.

That crack in the ceiling reminded me of myself—fractured but still holding. And I think of a woman in the bible named Miriam.

A woman who once led the nation in song, tambourine in hand, voice lifted in freedom. But later, when her voice was misunderstood, she was cast out. Silenced. And while Scripture says she stayed outside the camp for seven days, I wonder what it felt like inside her soul. Did she question everything? Did she replay what she said? Did she wonder if her voice would ever matter again?

That night didn't end with a dramatic decision. I didn't pack my bags. I didn't run. But I stayed—with myself. With my truth. I let the towel soak up my tears while I whispered every pain I hadn't spoken out loud. And in doing so, I claimed one fragile, trembling minute of healing.

Like Miriam outside the camp, I sat in a kind of exile—cut off not just from comfort, but from who I thought I was supposed to be.

And yet, there was something holy in that wilderness.

Because God didn't let the people move on without her. They waited.

And I wonder—what if God was doing the same for me?

Not pushing me away, but creating space to rebuild my voice, to realign my soul, to remind me that I still had a place in the camp... and in the story.

That's how it begins—not with a roar, but a refusal to abandon yourself again.

Miriam understood what it meant to have a voice—and what it felt like to be shut down.

She was a prophetess. A worship leader. A woman of vision and song. She danced with tambourines and led her people in praise after God parted the sea. But later, when she spoke up in ways others didn't understand, she was cast out. Sent beyond the camp. Separated for seven days. And while it's easy to read that as punishment, what speaks to me is this: the people waited for her return.

They didn't move on without her. Because her presence mattered. Her voice still held value. Her place in the story wasn't erased.

Miriam is the woman who lost her footing, questioned her role, and carried the weight of being misunderstood. But she was never disqualified. God still called her His. And I think of her when I reflect on my own silence—not the quiet of peace, but the kind where your voice has been dismissed for so long you start to believe it doesn't belong.

But if Miriam was restored… so, can we be.

There were so many moments I wanted to document every detail of what I'd endured. Every cruel word, every lie, every incident that made me question my sanity. But I didn't. I didn't want to give him that satisfaction. I knew he'd love it—he'd use it, twist it, make it his. And I couldn't let that happen. I wouldn't hand over my healing as ammunition. So instead of telling the world, I told the truth—to myself.

I wasn't crazy. I wasn't unstable. I wasn't too much.

It was just abuse.

And I had finally named it.

That was the beginning of my freedom. Because when you live in a gaslit world, naming what's real is holy work. It's resistance. It's reclaiming every inch of your soul the enemy tried to shrink.

One by one, I started to rewrite the narrative:

- I wasn't overreacting. I was responding to harm.

- I wasn't too emotional. I was deeply aware.

- I wasn't unstable. I was being destabilized.

- I wasn't broken. I was being broken down. And now?

- I'm rebuilding.

And I wasn't doing it alone.

God began to meet me in the moments I thought I had to hide. The bathroom floor. The tear-streaked car rides. The silent mornings where I couldn't form the words to pray, but I breathed them anyway. He met me there, in the stillness, not with condemnation, but compassion.

Scripture says, "Then you will know the truth, and the truth will set you free" (John 8:32). What it doesn't say—but what I now know—is that freedom rarely feels like a single breakthrough. Sometimes, it feels like slowly turning on the lights in a house you didn't know had grown dark. That house, for me, was my soul.

The enemy had crept into every room—twisting truth, distorting love, warping worth. And I had let him stay for far too long because I didn't know how to call it what it was.

But now? I walk those rooms with keys in hand.

Truth is the drywall. Prayer is the new paint. Forgiveness—of myself, not him—is the open window letting light back in.

I don't need the world to understand every detail of what I lived through. I don't even need to remember it all perfectly.

What I need is this: to trust myself again.

To know that if I say it hurt, it did. If I say it wasn't love, it wasn't. If I say I'm healing, I am. If I say I'm free, then let the record show—I'm walking out the front door with no apologies.

Learning to trust again after abuse is like learning to walk on a leg that was once broken. You move slowly. You doubt every step. You anticipate pain even when it's no longer there. You flinch at kindness. You wait for the rug to be pulled out from under you, even in safe places. And that's not because you're weak—it's because your body and soul are doing what they were trained to do: survive.

Our brains are wired for pattern recognition. It's one of God's most beautiful and complex gifts to us. Pattern-seeking helps us develop, grow, learn language, and navigate the world. But after abuse, those same neural pathways get hijacked by trauma. Your mind learns to expect rejection. Your body tenses when someone raises their voice, even if they're not yelling at you. You brace for betrayal, because that's what history has taught you.

But God begins where trauma ends.

He was there in my abandoned soul house.

Even when I thought the place inside me was too wrecked to be redeemed, too scared to be sacred, He entered anyway. While I boarded up emotional windows and hid in dark corners, He walked in like He owned the place—because He did. He had never left. And He wasn't scared off by the shattered glass or graffiti of shame written on the walls. He stepped in, shining His light through the broken windows, not to expose me, but to heal me.

He didn't demand I fix anything first. He didn't ask me to sweep the floors of pain or repaint the walls of regret. He simply said, "Let there be light." And in that light, I started to see the truth: I was never truly alone. He was there in my truths—the ones I whispered into pillows and scribbled into margins. The ones I questioned and tried to downplay. The ones that sounded too dramatic in my own head. He was there when I thought I was exaggerating. When I tried to rationalize his behavior. When I defended what broke me just to keep the peace. And He kept gently turning my face back toward the truth: "Daughter, you are not crazy. You are called. You are mine."

Even my notebook—where I logged days of abuse just to survive them— became holy ground. I used to think I was documenting my downfall. But really, I was testifying to my endurance. I wasn't keeping track of pain— I was witnessing my own strength. Every mark. Every page. Every line that said "I made it through another day" was an altar of remembrance. And God was in every word.

He met me there. In ink and in ache. In silence and in scribbles. The same God who met Hagar in the desert—the One who sees—was seeing me too. Not only when I sang worship or posted scripture. But when I was undone. When I collapsed on the floor with nothing to offer but a half-breathed "help me."

He was in the cracks of my foundation, not covering them up, but making them part of the story. Part of the pattern He was about to restore.

The same God who restored Miriam didn't wait for her to explain herself. He brought her back.

And I believe He was doing that for me—not erasing what happened but reintegrating me. Restoring me. Making room for me again.

Not as the woman I was in silence, but the woman I was becoming in truth.

Romans 12:2 says, "Do not conform to the pattern of this world, but be transformed by the renewing of your mind." I wasn't crazy—I was conditioned. And God was lovingly, patiently helping me rewrite the pattern.

He began renewing my mind—not just with truths about who He was, but with truths about who I was. That I was worthy of peace. That I could be loved without being controlled. That I didn't have to earn rest. That I could be fully known and still be fully safe.

When trauma taught me that love was conditional, God showed me His love was covenant. When abuse said my voice was too much, God reminded me it was meant to roar. When shame told me to hide, grace pulled me into the light.

And piece by piece, He helped me rebuild.

I no longer needed to write to prove what happened. I began writing to proclaim what God was doing now. My pen, once a tool of survival, became a weapon of truth.

It's funny how once you reclaim your voice, it starts to sound like worship again. Not the stage-and-microphone kind—but the battle-worn, desert-sung kind. The kind Miriam might've sung after rejoining the camp—low, steady, still sacred.

Because worship doesn't always mean singing praise in joy. Sometimes, it means choosing truth in pain.

The woman I am today still carries the weight of those years—but she no longer bows beneath it.

She walks upright. Keys in hand. Soul house no longer abandoned but inhabited by a holy presence that never left her, even when she left herself.

And if I ever doubt it again, I only need to return to the pages. Not to relive the pain, but to remember the truth: He was always there.

So, what do you do when your internal compass has been magnetized by manipulation?

You rewrite the pattern.

Not overnight. Not all at once. But intentionally.

Romans 12:2 says, "Do not conform to the pattern of this world, but be transformed by the renewing of your mind." This is the heart of healing after abuse. You don't just escape the toxic situation—you allow God to renew your thinking, to rebuild the foundation you now walk on. He rewrites the story that trauma tried to brand into your brain.

For me, that began with learning to trust myself again. And then—eventually—trusting others.

I started small. I asked myself basic questions each day:

- Am I safe right now?

- Is this person showing me consistency or confusion?

- Do I feel free to be myself, even when I'm not perfect?

These questions became checkpoints for truth. Not to make me paranoid—but to make me present. To give me space to pause and reflect instead of react. Abuse had trained me to anticipate harm. Healing invited me to expect peace.

When I was ready to trust again, it wasn't about trusting people first. It was about trusting God. I had to anchor my heart in something more solid than human behavior. Psalm 62:8 says, "Trust in Him at all times, you people; pour out your hearts to Him, for God is our refuge."

God became my baseline.

If I didn't know how to trust someone, I'd ask: Do they reflect the character of God? Are they patient, gentle, truthful, honoring, and consistent? Or do they manipulate, belittle, control, and confuse?

This is where discernment lives. Not in fear, but in faith-informed wisdom.

And while I was relearning trust, I also had to give myself permission to unlearn chaos.

Some of us were raised to think that love is loud. That drama equals passion. That anxiety is normal. But God doesn't work in confusion. Scripture tells us plainly in 1 Corinthians 14:33, "For God is not the author of confusion but of peace."

34

So, I stopped calling confusion "chemistry."

I stopped calling tension "excitement."

I stopped calling fear "intuition."

And I started calling peace what it is: holy.

Letting peace be my new normal didn't feel normal at first. In fact, it felt boring. Quiet. Soft. Almost suspicious. But that's how trauma heals— when you stop mistaking survival for stability and start allowing safety to settle into your nervous system.

I began creating new patterns:

- When I felt anxious, I breathed instead of apologizing.

- When I made a mistake, I forgave myself instead of spiraling.

- When someone offered love, I received it without bargaining.

These small acts became sacred. They weren't just habits. They were healing.

Psalm 16:11 says, "You make known to me the path of life; you will fill me with joy in your presence, with eternal pleasures at your right hand." That "path of life" isn't paved with pain. It's marked with joy. With clarity. With safety. And it's a path you get to choose now—minute by minute, step by step.

If you're learning to trust again, be gentle with yourself.

There will be moments when your gut screams run, and it's just your old wiring flaring up. There will be people who mean well but unknowingly trip your triggers. You'll want to crawl back into old patterns just because they feel familiar.

Don't judge yourself for that. Just don't stay there.

Because the woman you are becoming is not built from the wreckage—she is rising from it. And the more truth you walk in, the more peace you'll attract.

So, if trust feels hard, let this be your starting point: Trust the One who made you. Let His voice be louder than your fear. Let His peace override your panic. Let His word be the pattern you rebuild upon. Because when God rewrites your mind, He doesn't just erase the damage.

He redeems the entire narrative.

And that's where the new normal begins.

Love Bigger Challenge | Reclaim Your Voice

You are not too loud. You are not too much.

You are not broken for being bold.

You are simply remembering who you are.

When you've spent years being silenced, gaslit, or dismissed, reclaiming your voice can feel like rebellion. But it's not rebellion—it's restoration. Like Miriam, you may have been cast aside for speaking up.

But the truth is this: your voice is still yours, and it still belongs in the story.

Find a quiet space. Sit with turned to your Heart Notes.

Speak this truth out loud:

"My voice is sacred. My truth is sound.

God sees me. And I will not silence myself to be accepted."

Now, answer this prompt in your own words—uncensored, unfiltered:

What is one truth you silenced in order to survive?

Write it. Say it. Let it breathe.

Then take that truth and speak it aloud again—not to defend it, but to honor it. Even if your voice shakes. Even if no one else ever hears it.

Anchor Prayer | From Silence to Song

God,

I've spent too long second-guessing myself.

I've handed my truth to people who weren't worthy of it.

I've swallowed my voice to keep the peace,

and I've forgotten what it sounds like when I speak with courage.

But You have always known my voice.

You heard me in the bathroom floor whispers.

You remembered me outside the camp.

You waited while I wrestled.

Now, God—help me remember, too.

Help me trust what I know.

Help me honor what I feel.

Help me rise from silence not with shame,

but with sacred authority.

Restore my voice the way You restored Miriam.

Let me sing again. Let me speak again.

Let me tell the truth—even if only to myself.

Because I was never crazy. I was never too much.

I was just waiting for this moment.

Amen.

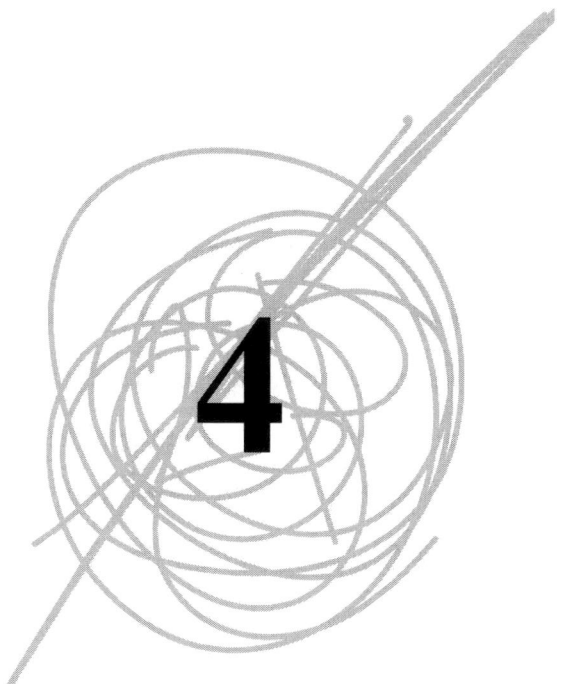

The Cost of Leaving—and the Worth of What's Next

"Forgetting what is behind and straining toward what is ahead, I press on toward the goal to win the prize…"—Philippians 3:13–14

Leaving cost me something.

That's the part people don't always talk about. When you finally break free from a toxic or abusive relationship, everyone wants to celebrate your strength. And yes—there is power in surviving, in saying "no more," in choosing peace over pain. But what many don't see is that freedom comes at a cost.

Even when you know it's the right decision. Even when you feel God's presence in your exit. Even when people clap for your courage—there is grief.

Not just grief for what happened. But grief for what you hoped it could've been.

Because somewhere in the middle of the mess, I had created a vision of what life might look like. I had poured myself into it. The house. The family. The business. The holidays. The tiny rituals that only made sense in that kitchen or on that porch. I wasn't just walking away from abuse— I was walking away from an entire life I tried to build out of broken bricks.

And I think that's why it hurt so much.

In those moments—those quiet, raw, disorienting moments after you leave—the grief hits in waves that make no sense.

You miss them… and you don't.

You remember good things… and wonder if they were ever real.

You ache for the family rhythm you created… even if it was built on instability.

You long for the version of life you thought you had… while knowing it almost destroyed you.

And your brain?

Your brain tries to make sense of it all.

Because that's what trauma-trained brains do: they seek patterns, closure, and something solid to stand on. But grief doesn't offer that right away. Instead, it offers fragments—memories you second-guess, flashbacks you didn't ask for, and questions that beg for clarity:

Was any of it real?

Did he ever love me?

Was I the crazy one all along?

How did I not see it sooner?

This is where the healing work begins.

Because in those moments, your brain is grieving, but your soul gets to speak the truth.

You get to become the narrator now. Not the one who gaslit you. Not the one who minimized your pain. Not the one who told half-truths and manipulated outcomes. You.

There were real memories.

The way we decorated the cookies at Christmas together—each of us huddled around the kitchen island, sticky fingers and icing-covered smiles—felt like something out of a movie. I still remember the way the lights from the tree glowed in the background while the kids tease each over who used too many sprinkles, and for a little while, the house felt soft. It felt like home.

There were spontaneous lake trips, too—the kind where we piled into the truck without a plan, stopped for gas-station snacks, played loud music with the windows down, and let the wind carry our laughter. Moments like that stitched themselves into my memory. Moments that looked like connection. Moments that felt like family.

Sometimes, we'd go get ice cream for the fifth night in a row. No one cared about the sugar or the mess or the chores waiting at home—we were just trying to hold onto a thread of joy. Watching everyone smile and laugh made me believe, if only for a moment, that maybe things were okay.

And the truth is… there was love.

In the cracks.

In the quiet.

In the stillness between storms.

There was love—in the moments it was safe enough to surface.

But love that only shows up when it's safe to do so isn't the kind of love that can sustain a life.

It was a love that tiptoed. A love that showed up after apologies, or in the "good weeks," where I behaved or when everything went according to his terms. It was laughter that lived on a timer. Joy that had to tiptoe through someone else's emotional minefield.

And that's what makes it all so complicated.

Because those moments were real. The cookies. The lake trips. The ice cream. The laughter.

But so was the fear that followed. So was the tension. The quiet punishments. The way joy always had a cost.

So, I learned to live for the highs and brace for the lows.

I became fluent in contradiction—how to feel happy while being afraid, how to create magic while tiptoeing through dysfunction, how to mother in a minefield. And I clung to those things.

Because when someone treats you terribly, but also occasionally treats you tenderly, your brain holds on to the tenderness like a life raft. You have to. That's how trauma bonding works. You begin to justify, minimize, compartmentalize. You separate the person from the pain because to see it all together would be too much.

So, when I left, I wasn't just grieving the harm. I was grieving the illusion.

The hope. The what-could-have-beens. The version of him I believed existed when he was being kind. The version of us I tried to hold together with my faith, my effort, my endurance.

But here's what I've learned: fantasy is not the same as faith. Faith is rooted in God's truth. Fantasy is built on what you hope someone will eventually become—usually at your own expense.

And that's why I think about Lot's wife.

Most of us only remember her for looking back. For that one moment when, as the city burned, she turned around and was turned into a pillar of salt. But what we rarely ask is: Why did she look?

Maybe it wasn't rebellion. Maybe it was grief. Maybe she wasn't longing for the wickedness she escaped, but for the version of her life she had built there. The home. The family rhythm. The sense of normalcy—even if it wasn't safe.

I get that. Because I've looked back, too. Not because I wanted to return, but because I wanted to make sense of what I was leaving behind.

Lot's wife reminds us of what happens when grief overtakes forward movement. When we get frozen in the ache. When we linger too long in what almost was.

But here's what I've learned: God's mercy isn't just in the rescue—it's in the redirection.

We don't walk away to be punished. We walk away so we can be restored.

And it took me a long time to tell myself that truth. Because I wanted it to be real. I wanted the investment to mean something. I wanted the good moments to outweigh the bad. I didn't want to believe that I had been living in something false for so long. That I had defended someone who would never do the same for me.

But telling the truth—to myself first—was the beginning of healing.

Letting go is not about bitterness. It's about honoring reality.

And that meant letting go of the dream I had for our family. Letting go of the vision I had spent six years building—one that included kids growing up together, family vacations, home renovations, shared traditions, even growing old together.

I let go of the version of him I built in my head—the version that would eventually "get it," would finally say sorry, would step into being the man I hoped he could be.

I let go of the belief that it was my job to fix it.

And that hurt.

It hurt like losing a future I had planned my entire heart around.

But as I grieved, I also started to see something else.

That leaving doesn't just cost you—it also clears the way.

It makes room for what's ahead.

Philippians 3:13–14 says, "…forgetting what is behind and straining toward what is ahead, I press on…" This doesn't mean we erase the past. It means we release it. We stop clinging to what was never meant to define us. We stop measuring our worth by what we couldn't fix. We stop shrinking to stay in places God has called us out of.

The truth is, I had to make peace with the cost in order to fully claim the worth of what's next.

Healing was hard. And confusing. Because grief and gratitude started showing up in the same room.

There were days I'd feel free and furious at the same time. Relieved and resentful. Empowered but exhausted. And that tension made me think I was doing it wrong. But healing isn't linear. It's layered.

And part of healing is rewriting the self-talk that trauma taught me.

Instead of saying, "I should've seen it sooner," I started saying, "I see it now—and that's what matters."

Instead of saying, "I failed my family," I began saying, "I saved my family from further damage."

Instead of saying, "I'm broken," I spoke aloud, "I'm being rebuilt."

God doesn't expect you to sprint into your new life without stumbling. He knows this is all new to you, too. That standing in your truth can feel like standing in a storm at first. That walking toward the future when the past is still whispering can feel like too much some days.

But you don't walk alone. Even when the odds are against you. Even when the enemy comes to tear you apart. You are not alone.

One of the first moments I knew I was stepping into something new was on a trip to Las Vegas with my girlfriends. It was a celebration of survival, of reclamation, of rediscovering who I was outside of the roles I'd been boxed into. And while it was supposed to be just fun and freedom, it ended up being something more:

It became a line in the sand.

I didn't just win healing that weekend.

I won a jackpot.

Literally.

In a moment so wild I could only call it divine humor, I hit big. And in that celebration—surrounded by friends, laughter, and lights—I felt something shift.

I had spent so long waiting for the other shoe to drop, so long surviving, that joy felt almost foreign. But that night, I let myself receive it. Not because I had earned it. But because I had made room for it.

And of course, the rumor mill churned.

Sometimes, when the truth threatens someone's image, a lie gets told instead. I remember a time when boundaries were enforced and someone didn't like it. Rather than accepting responsibility, they flipped the story—telling others I had made it all up just to cause trouble. That I was being dramatic. Vindictive. People repeated it. Some even believed it.

What hurt the most wasn't the lie itself—it was how quickly others accepted it without asking questions. How rumors became louder than facts. How silence was mistaken for guilt, and survival was twisted into manipulation.

That's the power of gaslighting: it shifts the focus away from what actually happened and turns the spotlight on the one who's already hurting. It teaches people to doubt what they saw, heard, or knew to be true. And after a while, even the truth-teller starts to wonder if maybe they are the problem.

But here's what I know now:

The truth doesn't need defending. It needs living.

So, I kept doing the right things. Kept telling the truth. Kept showing up for my kids. Kept holding space for healing. Because over time, people start to see through the smoke and mirrors. And the more I stood in integrity, the more the fog lifted—for me and for others.

Living the truth is worth what is next.

It hasn't been easy. I've lost people. I've lost places I once called home. I've lost illusions that were painful to part with.

But what I've gained?

Peace.

Clarity.

Self-trust.

A God who walks with me in every hallway of this new life.

I now understand that the cost of leaving was never meant to keep me from leaving. It was meant to remind me that the life I'm walking into is so valuable, it was worth losing everything that tried to keep me small. And on the days when the past still whispers, I don't silence it with shame—I respond with grace:

"Yes, it happened. But it doesn't define me."

"Yes, it hurt. But I don't live there anymore."

"Yes, I lost things. But I'm gaining so much more."

So, take heart, friend. If you've walked away from something that nearly broke you—if you're still carrying the weight of what was lost, still learning how to breathe freely again, still figuring out how to trust your own voice—know this: you are not alone. The grief is real. The healing is slow. But the worth of what's next is far greater than what you had to leave behind. This process—of telling the truth, of releasing the fantasy, of rewriting your self-talk and standing strong in your new beginning—is sacred. It is not easy, and it is not linear. But you are not behind. You are becoming.

And even now—even in this sacred undoing—God is not distant. He is not waiting for you to have it all figured out. He is not pacing on the other side of your healing, waiting for you to catch up. No—He is with you in this too. In every single moment.

In the seconds where you can barely catch your breath. In the minutes where all you've done is survive. In the days that blur with exhaustion and doubt. In the weeks where you question if you're making any progress. In the months when your soul still flinches at things it shouldn't have to. And in the years to come, when you're still untangling what was truth and what was trauma—He is there.

God is not only with you in your freedom. He was with you in the breaking. He's with you in the rebuilding. He's with you in every whispered prayer and shaky step. He is not ashamed of your process. He is not shocked by your grief. And He will not waste your pain.

You are not too late. You are not too far gone. You are not too much. You are not disqualified by what you endured. You are walking through—braver than you feel, stronger than you know—and you are not walking alone.

You are, step by step, one brave moment at a time, finding your way home.

And God is with you in this too.

In the seconds.

The minutes.

The days.

The weeks.

The months.

The years.

Still faithful. Still present. Still redeeming every piece of the story.

Love Bigger Challenge | Love the You Who Left

She didn't run because she was weak.

She walked because she was brave. And she deserves to be loved—by you. Leaving took everything. Not just strength, but surrender.

She didn't know what was on the other side. She only knew she couldn't stay. And that version of you—the one who walked away through the ache and the silence—needs to be seen. Not pitied. Not judged.

Loved. Boldly. Deeply. Fiercely.

Write a letter to the version of you who finally left.

Speak to her like a friend who saved your life—because she did.

Don't edit. Don't overthink. Tell her:

- What you see now

- What she taught you

- How proud you are

- Why her choice mattered

When you're done, choose one symbolic act of honor:

- Tuck the letter into your journal or Bible as a sacred reminder

- Burn it in a safe space as a holy release

- Read it aloud in your car or bathroom mirror

- Share it with a friend who's walking through their own leaving

- Fold it into an envelope and seal it—knowing she is covered in grace

Anchor Prayer | For the One Who Walked Away

God,

Thank You for giving me the strength to leave.

Even when I didn't feel strong.

Even when it didn't look brave from the outside.

Thank You for walking with me through every shaky step,

for steadying my soul when I didn't know what came next.

Today, I speak love over the woman who made that choice.

Not because she was perfect—

but because she was willing.

Willing to choose peace over pretense.

Healing over hiding.

Truth over fantasy.

She wasn't broken for walking away—

she was beginning again.

Help me honor her.

Help me love her like You do.

With compassion.

Without condition.

And with a heart full of grace for every step she took.

Amen.

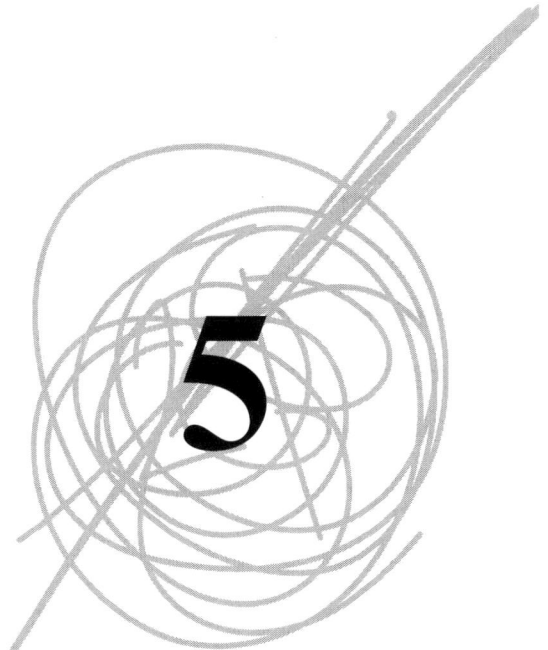

Trading Survival Mode for Sacred Surrender

"Come to me, all you who are weary and burdened, and I will give you rest." —Matthew 11:28

There are moments in life when the fog is so thick, you can't tell if you're standing still or moving forward. The weeks after we were kicked out weren't just uncertain—they were heavy with the weight of survival. But this time, instead of reacting, I found myself learning how to simply be. Not because I had all the answers, but because I had no other choice. We landed, not gracefully, but gratefully, at my parents' home. My boys and I had a bed to sleep in, even if it came with princess sheets from my childhood. It wasn't home, but it was safe. It was mercy in mattress form.

We didn't unpack; we exhaled. We didn't start over; we held still. The first weeks were blurry, but behind the blur was something real: the holy hush of survival surrendering into sacred rebuilding.

There were no instructions for this new life. Just instincts. Just grace. Just the rhythm of small, exhausted decisions strung together by faith. Court dates scribbled on sticky notes. Legal documents smudged with coffee rings and tears. My mornings were marked by the same mug of coffee reheated three times—never finished—because my mind couldn't hold still long enough to enjoy it. Every time I thought I might breathe, survival whispered, "Not yet."

But slowly, the ordinary became holy. Not easy. Not romantic. But sacred.

Our days were filled with recalibration. Finding our new normal.

My boys drove over forty miles each way just to stay in their school district—a tether to their old normal. Some days the car rides were filled with silence. Other days, with tired laughter. And once, with the sharp intake of panic when my oldest son was in a wreck on the highway. I rushed to him, heart racing, breath caught between fear and prayer. We made it through, but every week brought its own mountain.

Then, a promotion came. Unexpected. Undeserved in the eyes of the world but drenched in divine favor. It didn't just show up as a new role or a pay increase. It arrived like a sacred nod from heaven. A tangible reminder that God hadn't forgotten me. It felt like He pulled me aside in the middle of the storm, looked me in the eye, and whispered, "You are still My daughter, and I am still writing your story."

That promotion reminded me that I was like a modern-day Esther.

Not the royal robes or palace halls—but the quiet ache behind the crown.

The weight of being called up in a season where everything still hurt.

Esther didn't ask for influence. She didn't chase a title. She was chosen—and not just for favor, but for purpose. Her rise came in the middle of risk. In the tension between silence and boldness. In the moment when surrender meant everything.

That's what it felt like for me.

I didn't get promoted because life was perfect or because I had it all together. I got promoted in the middle of chaos. While still aching. Still healing. Still navigating court dates and whispered rumors.

And yet—God lifted me. Not to prove something. But to position something.

I didn't climb my way here—I was carried. And in that moment, I could almost hear it whispered:

"You were made for such a time as this."

Not despite your pain.

Not once everything is resolved.

But right here—in the middle of the mess.

That's the anointing of Esther.

And that's the kind of anointing I carry now, too.

That promotion was more than security—it was a marker of God's blessing. Not because life was easy now, but because favor isn't always about escape. Sometimes it's about endurance. It was as if God was showing me that even in the middle of brokenness, He was still building something beautiful.

But surrender isn't just about receiving miracles. It's about walking through the shadows of what you must face.

Healing meant confronting the man who had hurt me and my children. The man who twisted truth to protect his public image while privately dismantling mine. It meant hearing lies echo across bleachers and seeing judgment scroll through social media feeds. Someone once joked that maybe my son didn't win first place because my shoes weren't the right color—as if the bottom of my heels held the power to rewrite injustice. But I didn't flinch. I looked at my son, who showed up with nothing—no barn, no trailer, no advantage—just integrity and heart. That was the victory.

Because real victory isn't defined by ribbons or applause—it's defined by perseverance, by resilience, and by choosing love and dignity in the face of cruelty. That was the victory—because we chose to see it that way. Victory is born in the perspective we carry, not the approval we receive. Surrender was choosing silence when others gossiped. Surrender was showing up to livestock shows and school events even when whispers followed. I no longer needed to prove my worth or defend my story to people determined not to believe it.

I kept showing up. With shaky strength. With a tired smile. I packed lunches, pressed shirts, and kissed foreheads while grief and growth coexisted under the same roof. Each morning, I would send the boys off and sit and whispering, "God, just help me through today." Sometimes, that prayer came out as a sob. Sometimes, it was just breath.

But that unraveling? It made room for something sacred.

It didn't happen in church aisles or during worship songs. It happened on bathroom floors. In the front seat of my car, sitting on the patio late at night where I finally said, "I can't do this anymore," and meant it. I didn't need a stage. I needed a safe space to surrender.

So, I made calls. I shared my story. I let the tears come. I let my voice shake. And I listened when someone finally said, "You're not crazy. You're courageous."

Here's what I learned: surrender isn't weakness. It's wisdom. It's the invitation to stop pretending you can do it all and let God step in where you end.

It's saying, "God, I can't—but You can."

It's letting go of:

- The image I tried to protect.
- The fear I tried to manage.
- The weight I was never meant to carry alone.

In return, He gave me space to breathe again. Space to feel peace again. The silence that once terrified me became the soundtrack of healing. The breath I couldn't catch before became the exhale of grace.

Like the woman with the alabaster jar, I didn't show up with answers—I showed up with ache.

She didn't need to explain her past to the Pharisees. She just knelt at the feet of Jesus and poured out what she had. Her surrender was misunderstood by man but honored by God.

And that's how it felt in my own healing: my tears, my silence, my shaky prayers were sacred to Him—even when others dismissed them.

Jesus didn't shame her. He saw her. He called her forgiven. He called her worthy.

And I believe He says the same to us: "Your surrender is not weakness. It is worship."

Surrender is saying no to toxic people and yes to healthy boundaries. Surrender is giving up your need to explain your pain to people who only spectate it. Surrender is admitting that the path ahead might be unknown—but it's not unaccompanied.

And in that surrender, something beautiful grew.

No more criticism over laundry. No more fear about the sound of the garage door. No more racing heartbeats when the phone lit up. The silence that used to feel dangerous now felt like peace. My breath, once stolen by survival, now returned as praise.

I used to think the Proverbs 31 woman was unreachable. Perfect. Polished. Put-together.

But I see her differently now. She is strong because she surrenders. She laughs at the days to come because she trusts in the One who writes her future. She is clothed with strength and dignity not because she has it all together—but because she walks with God, even through the hard days.

I don't have to become her overnight. But I can become more like her, one surrendered moment at a time.

Proverbs 3:5-6 wrapped around me like armor: "Trust in the Lord with all your heart and lean not on your own understanding; in all your ways submit to Him, and He will make your paths straight."

I didn't need to see the whole path—I just had to take the next step. Some days, the step was as small as making the bed. Others, it was showing up at court. Sometimes, it was simply choosing not to reply to a hurtful message. But every step counted. Every surrender was sacred.

God didn't wait for me to clean up the mess. He met me right in it. In text messages from friends. In school lunches donated by strangers. In my boys' laughter. In my own breath.

And somewhere in those steps—unremarkable to the world, but holy to us—I stopped surviving.

I started becoming. Aligning my heart with God's will through surrender.

I choose to believe I wasn't broken. For years, I believed I was too damaged to ever feel whole again. But God whispered a new narrative: You're not broken. You're becoming. That mindset shift didn't erase the pain—but it reframed it. I was no longer someone to be fixed. I was someone being formed.

I traded in shame for curiosity. Instead of beating myself up for how long it was taking to heal or why I had stayed so long, I got curious. I asked, "What was I needing that I didn't know how to name?" Curiosity opened the door to compassion. Compassion unlocked grace.

I allowed myself to feel without judgement. I used to think emotions made me weak. But God created every tear, every deep breath, every ache of the heart. Feeling my pain was not a failure. It was faith in motion. Feeling is how we process. Feeling is how we release. And feeling is how we begin again.

And eventually, I began to believe: I wasn't just surviving.

I was becoming.

Live It Out Challenge | Sacred Surrender

Take a sacred pause.

Find a quiet moment—at the edge of your bed, in the car, on your porch with coffee still warm in your hands. This isn't about performing. It's about releasing.

Reflection + Journaling Prompt:

Turn to the Heart Notes section and draw two simple columns.

- On the left, title it: Release

- On the right, title it: Reclaim + Surrender

Under Release, write what you're ready to let go.

Fear. Shame. Control. Comparison. The lies that no longer serve you.

Under Reclaim + Surrender, write what God says is yours.

Peace. Identity. Joy. Strength. Faith. Purpose.

Now circle one from each list—and sit with them. Let your body feel the difference. Let your heart catch up to your hope.

Speak this truth out loud:

"I don't have to carry what was never mine. I am safe to surrender—and strong enough to receive."

Anchor Prayer | For the Moment I'm Ready to Let Go

God,

I've carried so much for so long.

Some of it wasn't even mine to hold—

expectations, pressure, shame, fear.

But I don't want to live in survival mode anymore.

Today, I release what's too heavy, and

I receive what You've promised.

Trade my control for Your peace.

My striving for Your presence.

My fear for Your steady hand.

Help me walk in sacred surrender—not because I'm giving up,

but because I'm giving it to You.

Amen.

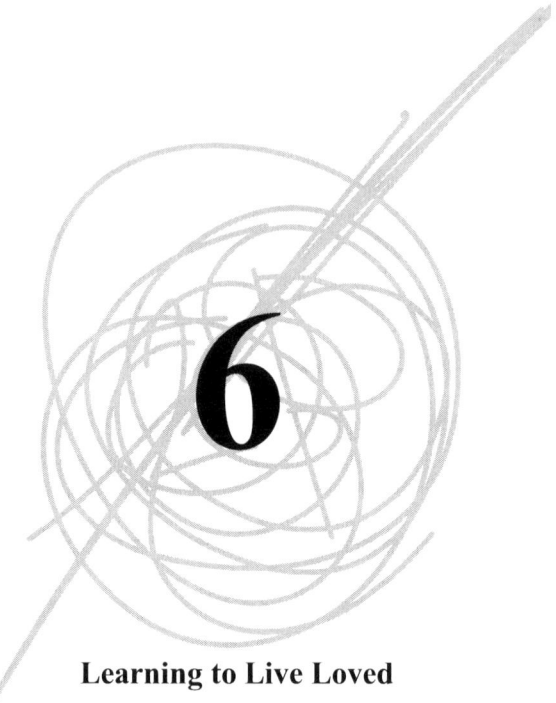

Learning to Live Loved

"For I am convinced that neither death nor life, neither angels nor demons, neither the present nor the future, nor any powers... will be able to separate us from the love of God that is in Christ Jesus our Lord." — *Romans 8:38–39*

To live unloved is to live disconnected from the truth of who you are—who God created you to be. His design for you has always been rooted in love. Before the first wound, before the first lie, before anyone else had the chance to define you—He already did. And His definition has never changed: Beloved. Chosen. Seen.

Living unloved feels like constantly questioning your value, second-guessing your every word, and shrinking your light so someone else doesn't feel threatened by your brightness. It keeps you apologizing for your presence, for your voice, for your needs. And eventually, it convinces you that survival is the same thing as living. It convinces you that love must always come with conditions, punishment, or performance.

But that is not the love of God. His love isn't earned—it's inherited. It's not withheld when you fail. It's not revoked when you stumble. It's the kind of love that runs to meet the prodigal, that clothes the wounded with worth, that silences the shame and sings identity over you.

But that is not the love of God.

When we left, we had nothing but a couple of bags of clothing. There wasn't time to take any of our personal items—no keepsakes, no school supplies, no beds or furniture. Just the bare minimum we could carry. For months, we had no idea where our belongings were. Eight months after walking away, we were finally told where everything had been stored. By then, we had already learned to live without it. The ache of that reality had long settled into our bones.

That kind of loss changes you. It strips away more than possessions—it unravels the story you thought you were living. And it forces you to ask a new question: Who am I without everything I built around me?

That question became the turning point for me. It didn't come with lightning bolts or a flashing banner. It came in quiet moments. In the stillness of borrowed spaces and the chaos of court dates. And it led me to a decision that shifted the course of my healing: I chose to finish my doctorate.

And I believe God smiled—not because I was proving anything, but because I was reclaiming something holy. I was walking in His design. I wasn't earning His approval. I was reflecting His glory—simply by rising again.

Not to prove a point to anyone else. But to prove something to myself.

I chose to love myself enough to honor a dream that existed long before the chaos. Even in the midst of rebuilding. Even with the weight of fear and uncertainty. I wrote research papers in stolen minutes—on the floor, at the kitchen counter, at red lights with my laptop open in the passenger seat.

It wasn't about achieving something external. It was about reclaiming something internal. That degree became more than a milestone—it became a symbol of self-worth resurrected. A personal commitment that whispered: I still matter.

That whisper—that inner truth—became a lifeline in the days that followed. Because learning to live loved meant I had to first confront all the ways I had lived unloved. It meant recognizing the trauma that told me love had to be earned. It meant learning how to receive without guilt. And that journey began, not with clarity, but with surrender.

The months after leaving weren't measured in traditional ways. Time blurred. Days melted into each other, tracked more by court dates, and sleepless nights. We were technically "living" with my parents, but it never felt like living—it felt like floating.

And though I didn't always feel it, I now see it: God was sustaining us in the shadows. He was the thread in our borrowed blankets, the stillness in our chaos, the Provider in every small mercy. He was rebuilding me from the inside out, starting with breath.

I kept a tote in the back of the car with just the essentials—our toothbrushes, a couple of pairs of jeans, and my golf clubs. It never felt settled, but it was close enough, and we were just grateful to be safe.

I was working full-time and coming home to do homework for my doctorate at night. Most of the time, I did assignments sitting cross-legged on the floor or perched at the kitchen counter, trying not to cry into my keyboard. My boys were growing, needing structure—but all I had to offer was love, reassurance, and a desperate kind of consistency: frozen pizza on Tuesdays, gas station chocolate milk on Fridays, and prayer every single night.

We had no access to our old life—no bedrooms to call their own, no dresser drawers to open. Their fishing poles were still locked away in a garage we knew nothing about. Their belt buckle collection, the lucky penny they'd saved, baby pictures, blankets, report cards—everything that reminded them of home—was somewhere we couldn't reach.

So, we started over.

And slowly, we stitched together a new version of "normal."

But it was ours.

It wasn't glamorous. It wasn't pretty. But it was real—and it was healing. In those months, we didn't just survive—we became stronger. Starting over wasn't a single moment. It was a million tiny decisions to keep going when everything told us we couldn't.

Decisions like getting out of bed when staying under the covers seemed safer. Texting a friend back even when I didn't want to talk. Sitting in the school parking lot just to make sure my boys got through the day. Choosing to pray when I had more questions than answers. Washing dishes while replaying painful conversations and choosing not to let bitterness take root. Writing a sentence for my dissertation when my hands were shaking. Letting myself laugh at a joke. Saying "I love you" without fear of being manipulated.

But even as we rebuilt, shame still lingered like smoke. It crept into quiet car rides and whispered in grocery store aisles. Trauma had trained my brain to equate love with punishment, affection with control, safety with silence. And when love did show up—kind, safe, patient—I didn't always trust it. I wasn't sure how to live inside love that didn't ask me to shrink.

I think of Gomer, the woman who kept running back to places of shame—and the God who kept calling her home. Her story wasn't pretty. She was messy. Unfaithful. Rejected. But God instructed Hosea to pursue her—not as punishment, but as a picture. A picture of how He loves us. Not once. But always. Not because we deserve it. But because love is who He is.

I'm Gomer some days—unsure if I can be fully known and still fully accepted. But God doesn't flinch. He doesn't walk away. He clothes me in grace and whispers: You are Mine.

Learning to live loved wasn't a light switch moment. It was a slow unlearning. A steady retraining. A quiet rewriting of everything I believed about my worth.

I had to learn that my value wasn't tied to how useful, agreeable, or quiet I could be. God had already called me beloved before I ever earned a thing.

Living loved looked like letting myself exhale fully. Like not rereading a text message twenty times to decode it. Like not apologizing for crying.

Like making dinner and dancing in the kitchen just because the music was on.

It meant saying no without guilt. Saying yes without fear. Choosing people who made space for my healing—not just my strength.

But more than anything, learning to live loved meant learning to stop performing and start abiding. To stop running for approval and start resting in truth.

It meant filtering my emotions through God's purpose—not the other way around.

Emotions are real—but they're not always right. Emotions may rise like waves, but purpose anchors you. When I felt unworthy, I reminded myself: I am chosen. When I felt invisible, I repeated: I am seen. When I felt too broken, I declared: I am whole in Christ.

Fear may feel familiar, but it's not from God.

Scripture is clear: "For God has not given us a spirit of fear, but of power and of love and of a sound mind." (2 Timothy 1:7)

Fear tells you to hide. Love calls you to show up. Fear says you'll fail. Love whispers: I'm with you.

God's love is not unpredictable like human love. It is not based on mood or merit. His Word says He is "the same yesterday, today, and forever" (Hebrews 13:8). When your nervous system braces for chaos, He offers peace. When trauma says brace for impact, God says, "Be still and know" (Psalm 46:10).

And joy—real, deep joy—is love in motion. Joy is not a product of perfection; it's the fruit of presence. It's not the absence of struggle—it's the awareness of God with us in it.

I started practicing joy not when everything was fixed, but when I realized I was already held.

Joy was lighting a candle. Joy was laughing at dinner. Joy was watching my boys sleep peacefully, knowing no one would yell at them in the morning. Joy didn't always feel loud—but it always felt free.

In that freedom, I began to love myself not for what I could do or how I could perform—but for who I was becoming. I wasn't just rebuilding a life. I was reclaiming a heart.

Love started looking like boundaries. Like honest conversations. Like canceling plans to rest. Like praying not because I had the words, but because I believed God was listening.

One day, my youngest son said, "Proud of you mom."

That was the moment.

I didn't need a relationship to validate me. I didn't need approval from people who didn't know my story. I didn't need a stage or spotlight.

I needed to live loved. Fully. Freely. Unapologetically.

And just when I thought I had to earn my way back into joy—He whispered, "Daughter, you were never out of reach."

Pause there. Because nothing—not abandonment, not fear, not the lies you believed—has ever separated you from the love of God.

Romans 8:38–39 says, "Nothing can separate us from the love of God." And that includes shame. Fear. Mistakes. Abandonment. Betrayal. Nothing.

If God calls me loved, then I have permission to live like it.

Not timid. Not rehearsed. But rooted.

And not only are you loved—you are called to be love.

You have permission to live like it, too.

This kind of love is not loud or boastful. It's consistent. It's patient. It's reflective of grace. Living loved means carrying that love into every room you walk into—into every hard conversation, every new relationship, every quiet night where doubt creeps in. It means reclaiming who God says you are, even when the mirror shows a version of you still healing.

To live loved is to live with courage. It's a decision—repeated daily—to trade shame for significance, fear for freedom, and performing for presence. It's declaring over your life: I am already loved, so I will move in love. I will lead with love. I will receive love.

So, make the commitment. To believe it. To walk in it. To reclaim it with every courageous breath. You don't have to earn it. Just receive it. Let your life be the evidence.

Live. Loved.

Live It Out Challenge | Live Like You're Already Loved

You don't have to perform for love. You don't have to earn what God has already given. Today, let love lead—not fear, not shame, not the old patterns that taught you to hide. In your Heart Notes section, create two simple columns:

- Left Side: Lies Love Is Not

    o Love is not fear

    o Love is not silence

    o Love is not punishment

    o Love is not earned

    o Love is not shrinking to fit someone else's comfort

- Right Side: What God's Love Truly Is

    o Love is safe

    o Love is unconditional

    o Love is empowering

    o Love is healing

    o Love is a reflection of God's heart

Now choose one truth from the right side and commit to walking in it today. Write it on your mirror. Speak it out loud. Let it interrupt the lies that still whisper to your soul. Then ask yourself gently: What would it look like if I lived today like I am already loved?

Anchor Prayer | Walk in the Love That's Already Yours

God,

I don't want to perform for love anymore.

I want to receive it—freely, fully, without fear.

Remind me that I don't have to earn what You've already given.

When shame rises, speak truth.

When fear whispers, anchor me in Your presence.

Teach me to walk in love that is safe, steady, and Yours.

Let today be shaped by grace, not guilt—

by belonging, not striving.

I am already loved.

Help me live like it.

Amen.

This Is What Healing Looks Like

"I will restore to you the years that the locusts have eaten." —Joel 2:25

Years later, I look back and barely recognize the woman I used to be. The one who flinched at footsteps. Who timed her showers to avoid punishment. Who whispered affirmations into the silence just to prove to herself she was still alive. Who counted days in circles. That version of me lived moment to moment, in a kind of invisible war zone, surviving on grit and prayer and the smallest embers of hope.

That war zone wasn't metaphorical. It was real. I remember the night he chased me down the hallway, his rage echoing off the walls, and I— desperate for evidence, for truth to be seen—hit record on my phone.

That one act, that tiny bit of rebellion, triggered an explosion. A metal cup hurled at me with full force, and it struck my lower back. The pain took me to my knees, but what cut deeper was the hatred in his eyes. I wasn't a person in that moment. I was a threat. A threat to the false narrative, to control, to power. And yet, even in that moment, I whispered to myself, "You are still here. Keep breathing."

That kind of fear rewires your brain. It conditions you to constantly anticipate harm, to expect punishment just for existing. And once you're free, that wiring doesn't disappear overnight. Healing begins not in the absence of danger, but in the presence of safety. It starts in the subtle shift from bracing to breathing.

I think of the woman who bled for twelve years—rejected, exhausted, isolated, and out of options. She didn't arrive to Jesus with strength. She arrived on the ground, reaching from behind, believing that if she could just touch His robe, healing would come.

And it did.

But before He healed her body, He turned around to see her. Really see her. And He called her "Daughter."

That's what healing in years feels like sometimes. You spend so long being defined by the pain that you forget your name. But Jesus doesn't. He sees the reach. He honors the faith. And He restores your identity before anything else.

But healing isn't loud. It doesn't arrive with flashing lights and a soundtrack. Healing in years is a quiet process. It creeps in on tiptoe. It moves like mist over broken ground. It doesn't erase the past—but it reclaims it. It restores you piece by piece, decision by decision, moment by moment.

Healing in years looks like walking into a room and not scanning for exits. It looks like standing in a store aisle and realizing you don't have to ask permission to choose the color of a towel. It's reaching for the white one, because you like it, and that's enough. It's driving down the road without white-knuckling the steering wheel every time your phone buzzes. It's not explaining your joy. It's sleeping through the night. It's laughing until your stomach hurts. It's breathing, not bracing.

It's standing in front of a room full of women—chin high, voice steady—sharing your story not as a victim, but as a vessel of victory. It's being both soft and strong, broken and beautiful. It's knowing the cracks didn't ruin you—they became the way the light got in.

It's celebrating your son's livestock wins knowing you once questioned if he'd ever show again. It's hearing their laughter echo through a home you created from nothing. Watching them dig through a drawer full of their own things and knowing there was a time they wondered, if they would ever have their things again. It's saying, "We are loved, we are safe, and we matter."

It's closing your laptop after submitting your final doctoral paper—done from a kitchen table you put back together after it was taken apart in a million pieces out of spite—and whispering, "We did it," to a quiet house that finally feels like peace. It's letting tears fall because you're no longer afraid of the quiet. You are no longer afraid of yourself.

That's what healing looks like—finding your purpose, standing in it fully. I found mine in sharing my story with other women healing like me. I prayed over high domestic violence areas in our town. I volunteered at homeless shelters, sent books to women in need of healing, and wrote this book. I shattered being a victim and turned my healing into my greatest strength. Purpose doesn't arrive when everything is perfect—it awakens when you decide your pain won't be wasted.

God didn't ask me to be impressive. He asked me to be His. Before I ever spoke on a stage, volunteered, or wrote a chapter, He already called me worthy. His love wasn't waiting for me on the other side of my healing—it was the lifeline that got me there.

Isaiah 43:1 says, "Do not fear, for I have redeemed you; I have summoned you by name; you are mine."

That's what love does. It doesn't rush you. It roots you.

Healing in years means you stop performing and start belonging—to yourself, to your children, to God. It means you build a life not from what was lost, but from what you never knew was possible. It means every fear-based belief gets rewritten. Every lie that said you were too broken, too late, too much, or not enough gets replaced with truth: You are still here. And that is proof that restoration is real.

Healing isn't linear. It moves in spirals. In some seasons, you're running. In others, you're crawling. Sometimes the victory is submitting a dissertation. Sometimes it's just getting out of bed and brushing your teeth. One is not more holy than the other.

For me, the healing came not just in the milestones, but in the mundane. In washing dishes without waiting to be criticized. In buying the name-brand cereal just because my boys like it. In letting the house be messy because joy doesn't require perfection. In lighting a candle. In laughing at a movie. In staying up late with a friend without guilt.

Healing looked like trusting people again. Letting safe hands hold my story. Relearning how to accept kindness. Letting someone open a door for me without assuming it came with conditions. Allowing love to return—not as rescue, but as partnership.

And yes, healing meant grieving, too. Grieving the years lost to fear. The innocence that was taken. The holidays that were heavy. The love that wasn't safe. Grief became part of my healing—because you cannot reclaim what you don't first admit was taken.

The story of Hannah comes to mind. A woman in the bible who knew the ache of unfulfilled desire. The sting of being misunderstood. The shame of being seen as less than.

She didn't suppress her pain—she poured it out.

Scripture says she prayed in "bitterness of soul." She wept. She couldn't even form words—only her lips moved. And people judged her for it. Thought she was drunk. Misread her grief.

But God didn't.

God met her there. In her barrenness. In her breakdown. And in that sacred moment, He didn't just promise her a child—He reminded her that her sorrow wasn't the end of her story.

Healing, like Hannah's, doesn't always come quickly. But it comes. And when it does, it doesn't just change your circumstances—it transforms your soul.

I had to grieve the woman I didn't get to be sooner. The mother I couldn't be when I was too busy surviving. The version of myself that used to apologize for everything. I wrapped her in grace. I thanked her for getting us through. And I let her rest.

Because now, I am becoming.

Becoming the woman who trusts her gut. Becoming the mother who laughs loud and is filled with love. Becoming the daughter who doesn't flinch when the phone rings. Becoming the friend who isn't afraid to speak truth or ask for help. Becoming the leader who shows up—not in perfection, but in presence.

This is what healing looks like. Not polished. Not linear. But sacred.

Healing in years looks like finally believing you deserve to be happy—and then fighting for that happiness with gentleness and grit. It's seeing your reflection in the mirror and smiling instead of scanning for flaws. It's journaling not just about the pain, but about the possibilities. It's falling asleep without fear. It's waking up with purpose.

Healing in years is watching your children run into a home where they are not afraid, where they know, laughter doesn't have to end in yelling. It's having a quiet evening with a book and realizing that silence no longer feels dangerous—it feels like peace. It's surrounding yourself with people who remind you of your worth, who speak truth over your weariness, who hold your hands on the hard days and dance with you on the good ones.

If you're not there yet—if you're still in the middle of it—please know that this healing is still yours.

It's waiting for you.

It's unfolding, slowly, steadily, beautifully. And if you have started to glimpse this kind of healing, celebrate it. Don't downplay your growth. Don't minimize your becoming. You made it here on purpose, with purpose.

Give yourself grace to get there if you aren't. Celebrate it boldly if you have. You are living proof that healing is holy.

Maybe today you're reading this while sitting in a borrowed space, wondering how long you'll be in limbo. Maybe the noise of the past still echoes in your bones, and you're just trying to make it through the next hour.

Let me whisper this into your moment: it won't always feel like this.

One day, you'll buy flowers just because you want them on your table.

One day, you'll laugh so hard your sides ache—and you won't second-guess the joy.

One day, you'll make dinner without flinching at the sound of footsteps. You'll sleep without keeping one ear open. You'll pick out clothes without fearing what someone else will think.

One day, you'll walk into a room and feel safe.

You'll make your coffee the way you like it, sit on your porch in the morning light, and say, "This is mine. This life is mine."

One day, your tears will be from laughter. Your prayers will be full of praise. Your children's eyes will shine with the safety they now know.

One day, you'll dance again.

And you'll realize: you're not surviving anymore. You're living. Fully. Freely. Loved.

Sometimes, I imagine sitting across from the version of me who first whispered, "I think I need to leave."

I'd take her hand. Look her in the eye. And I'd say:

"You were never too much. You were never too late. You were never alone. I see you now—braver than you ever believed. And I'm living in the life you made possible."

She might not believe me right away. But I'd tell her to keep going anyway.

Because healing in years doesn't just restore what was lost. It makes space for a life you couldn't have imagined when you were surviving.

And when you get there? You'll know.

You'll recognize the peace. The stillness. The sacred quiet that used to scare you.

You'll walk through the door of your own life and say, "I'm home."

Not because everything is perfect.

But because now, you're free.

Love Bigger Challenge | Declare It

This week, choose a quiet space to speak truth over your present self—
not the woman you used to be, but the one standing here today.

In the Heart Notes section of your book, write a letter that affirms her:

- Speak to her strength.

- Celebrate the places she's healed.

- Honor the ones still tender.

- Remind her she's worthy of love—not because she's "fixed," but
  because she's still here. Still becoming. Still brave.

When you're done, read it out loud. Let your own voice carry truth back
to your soul. Then fold the letter and tuck it somewhere sacred—a
journal, a Bible, your nightstand drawer.

Return to it whenever the whispers of shame try to distort your reflection.

Because healing isn't just surviving—it's declaring:

"I am worth living for. I am worth loving now."

Anchor Prayer | Speak, Lord—I'm Listening

God,

Thank You for walking with me through every storm.

I no longer need to hide from myself—

because You've already seen me and called me worthy.

Speak truth over the parts of me that still carry shame.

Silence the voices that say I am too much or not enough.

Let Your words be louder than my fears.

Help me see myself through Your eyes—

Not as broken, but becoming.

Not as too late, but right on time.

Not as a project, but as a promise You're fulfilling.

I declare today: I am worth healing.

I am worth loving.

I am worth living for.

And I believe You are still writing beauty into my becoming.

Amen.

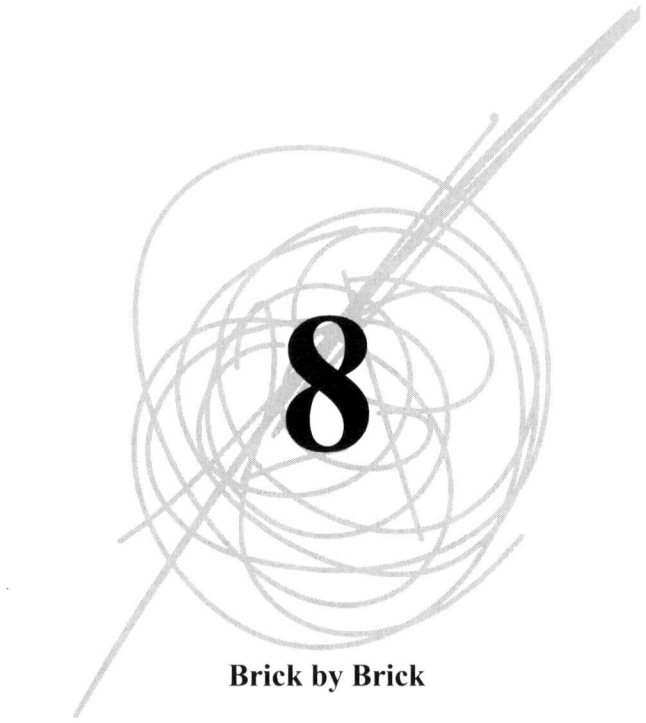

8

Brick by Brick

"They all plotted together to come and fight against Jerusalem and stir up trouble against it. But we prayed to our God and posted a guard day and night to meet this threat." —Nehemiah 4:8-9

Long before I ever realized how much the story of Nehemiah would mirror my own healing, his courage laid the foundation. Nehemiah wasn't a warrior or builder by trade. He was a cupbearer—a servant in the king's court. But when he heard that the walls of Jerusalem had crumbled, his heart broke. He prayed. He fasted. And then, with the king's blessing and God's calling, he returned to lead the effort to rebuild what had been destroyed. He didn't wait for perfect weather or a pristine worksite. He rebuilt with broken stones, burned gates, and opposition from all sides. Still, he kept building—one hand on the bricks, the other gripping his sword.

Healing doesn't always begin with beauty. Sometimes it starts in the dust—in the silence after the collapse, with smoke still rising from the ashes of what was. When we left, I didn't walk into healing with clarity. I walked into survival. I didn't have a plan or polished path. I had bruised hope, a couple of bags of clothing, a car full of kids and questions, and a God who hadn't let go.

Like Nehemiah surveying the broken walls of Jerusalem, I stood at the edge of my life, taking in the damage. Shame tried to rush in, but I remembered Nehemiah didn't run from the rubble—he walked it. He examined it. He prayed over it. And then he built.

So did I.

I wasn't handed a new blueprint for life. I was handed a thousand broken pieces. Court orders. Less than ideal living arrangement. Frozen bank accounts. Children asking if they could have their things back. I couldn't give them what they lost. But I could give them what was left of me. And I could build.

Before I ever knew how to rebuild, Ruth showed me what rebuilding could look like. Her story is often romanticized as a love story—and yes, there's a Boaz. But before there was redemption, there was devastation. Ruth didn't begin with restoration. She began with loss.

She was a Moabite widow. A foreigner. A woman who had every reason to walk away from the ruins of her life and start over somewhere easier. And yet, when given the choice, she said something sacred to her mother-in-law Naomi:

"Where you go, I will go. Where you stay, I will stay. Your people will be my people and your God my God."

(Ruth 1:16)

That was not the language of comfort. That was the language of covenant. Ruth made a brave, grief-soaked decision to walk into the unknown. She left the only life she had known—not with a plan, but with faith.

When she and Naomi arrived in Bethlehem, they had nothing but each other. No home. No inheritance. No certainty. And what did Ruth do? She rose early. She went out into the fields to glean—picking up leftover barley behind the harvesters. She gathered scraps. She worked humbly. Quietly. Consistently. She rebuilt not by striving for status, but by showing up to the sacred in front of her.

And that's how I felt in my own healing. Like Ruth, I wasn't building a mansion. I was gathering scraps—of energy, of faith, of courage. I was trying to survive emotionally and spiritually while rebuilding something that resembled a life. I wasn't walking into a field of abundance—I was walking into a field of trauma, hoping that maybe something good could grow.

I remember waking up to emails from lawyers, scrambling to finish assignments, trying to make it to work on time, praying my sons didn't feel the emotional aftershock I was barely surviving. I didn't have clarity. I didn't have closure. But I had one thing:

I showed up.

And showing up was sacred.

Just like Ruth didn't know Boaz would notice her, I didn't know if anyone would see the quiet grit I carried. I didn't know if my faithfulness in the unseen places would ever amount to anything. But God knew. He always knows.

God honors the gleaners. The women who rise and go. The ones who don't wait for the conditions to be perfect, but choose to step into purpose anyway. The ones who are willing to be vulnerable. Willing to work. Willing to believe healing is possible even while your hands still shake. Ruth didn't ask for recognition—she asked for mercy. And Boaz, upon seeing her, didn't just admire her work ethic. He saw her character. Her courage. Her kindness. And then he spoke the blessing over her that still echoes today:

"May the Lord repay you for what you have done. May you be richly rewarded by the Lord, the God of Israel, under whose wings you have come to take refuge." (Ruth 2:12)

When I read those words in my own season of rebuilding, I wept. Because I wasn't asking for favor. I was just asking for peace. But God, in His mercy, gave me both.

Like Ruth, I didn't have control over the outcomes. But I could control my obedience. I could keep showing up for my boys. I could keep choosing kindness when bitterness felt easier. I could keep finishing my doctorate, folding socks, cooking dinner, and brushing tears off my cheeks when no one was watching.

And little by little, like barley in the field, God gave me handfuls on purpose. Not because I earned it—but because He is faithful.

Because what if the rubble wasn't the end but the beginning of something sacred? What if, instead of looking for a whole plan, I learned to trust the next step?

What if the rubble wasn't the end but the blueprint?

Healing began when I stopped asking why the wall came down and started asking what God could build with what remained. I realized that God doesn't need a clean slate to create something holy. He uses what we bring—even if it's dust and tears.

Just like Nehemiah faced mockers who said, "What are those feeble Jews doing?" I heard the voices—internal and external. "She'll never make it." "She's just looking for attention." "You can't raise boys without him." The worst voice was my own.

But I prayed. I showed up. And I started laying bricks.

One day, one choice at a time.

One hand on the work, one hand on the sword.

Nehemiah instructed his people to build with one hand and hold a weapon in the other. That's what healing looked like for me. I rebuilt while staying alert. I laid down shame and picked up truth. I laid down fear and picked up boundaries. I built a bedtime routine with my boys, and I guarded my peace like my life depended on it—because it did.

I remember standing in the school gym ready for the homecoming pep rally, still trembling from a court hearing that morning. I breathed deep, fixed my face, and walked in. Brick.

I bought new beds for my boys, so they'd have something comforting to sleep on. Brick.

I took a different route to work because I found out he was using my commute to track me. Sword.

I started counseling. Brick.

I learned how to block and bless—block harmful access, bless my future anyway. Brick. Sword. Brick. Sword.

Even so, I was still mocked for my efforts to build a better life for my family.

Just the same, Nehemiah's enemies tried to pull him down off the wall with distractions and accusations. Rumors swirled. Lies circulated. Social media became a weapon in the hands of people who only knew a piece of the story. People speculated why we left, where we went, how we could possibly make it.

I remember seeing a post—a bracelet with a date that came before I had even left. It wasn't loud, but it said enough. In that quiet moment, I felt the weight of reality shift. While I had been holding on, praying things might change, a different story was already unfolding. It wasn't just the post—it was what it represented. A turning point. A heartbreak. A release. And still, I chose to stay grounded. I stayed on the wall.

And eight months after we left, we were finally told where our belongings had been taken. I prepared myself to find nothing—but by God's grace, we were able to recover some keepsakes. Most of it was destroyed or dismantled. I don't know who handled the items or why choices were made, but I do know this: that season revealed a lot—not just about others, but about me. The pain refined my purpose. What felt like loss became a moment of clarity, a sacred reminder of who I am and what I still carry.

And then, another miracle: we bought our own home. A real home. Our safe place. A fresh start. A space to rebuild—not just structure, but identity, belonging, and peace. That house became the physical manifestation of every prayer, every tear, every brick laid in faith.

We tracked our progress the way Nehemiah likely did—with faith and focus. I celebrated the first time I made it through a whole week without crying at work. The first time, my boys hugged me without fear of ridicule. The first night, I fell asleep without reliving the trauma.

Each moment of peace was sacred ground. Each one a reminder: We were still here. And we were building.

You don't have to feel strong to be strong.

You don't need a perfect five-year plan to walk in purpose.

You don't have to see the whole story to start rebuilding.

You just have to get up and glean.

You just have to show up—to therapy, to that hard conversation, to the court date, to the bathroom mirror where you say, "I am still here." That is the field. That is the sacred. That is the work.

Ruth teaches us that sometimes favor finds us in the field, not in the spotlight.

Her legacy wasn't forged in luxury. It was formed in loyalty.

And her faithfulness—quiet, gritty, sacrificial—positioned her in the very lineage of Jesus.

You don't have to do anything flashy to be used by God. You just have to be faithful with what's in front of you.

That's how walls are rebuilt. That's how healing happens.

I prayed in courtrooms and cried in gas station parking lots. I journaled prayers like Nehemiah drafted plans. I asked God not just for relief but for wisdom. And little by little, the wall went up. Not a wall of hiding. A wall of healing.

There were days I wanted to quit. Days when the work of healing felt heavier than the pain that caused it. Days when the bricks slipped from my hands, and I just sat in the rubble and wept.

But I learned that God doesn't expect us to build without breaks. He only asks that we don't walk away.

So, I stayed. I rested when needed. I stepped back when overwhelmed. And then I picked up the next brick.

I remember rebuilding in the hidden, holy spaces no one else could see. Not grand declarations—just quiet, sacred moments. Like folding tiny socks beside my son, the room humming with unspoken comfort. Or sipping morning coffee across from my mom, both of us wrapped in a silence.

I remember helping my boys clean out their trucks, wash their football jerseys, and make their beds—not because I had to, but because sometimes love whispers through acts of service and the scent of clean linen. No explanation needed. No words required.

And then there was the day the tears came—uninvited, unstoppable. But I let them. I didn't rush to hide or tidy myself up. I just cried… in front of them. And they didn't flinch. They stayed.

And in their staying, I started to believe again—maybe I was still worthy of being seen. Still worthy of love.

Sometimes the bricks looked like boundaries: learning to say no without guilt, declining phone calls that led to emotional spirals, learning to turn my phone off at night to protect my peace. Other times, the bricks were moments of radical grace—taking my kids to play golf even when I wanted to cry, laughing during a movie night even if the day had started with tears.

And if you're reading this, maybe your brick today is just getting out of bed. Maybe it's texting a friend and saying, "I need help." Maybe it's turning worship music on while you fold laundry or applying for that job even though you're scared to start over.

Rebuilding isn't glamorous. It's not about perfect aesthetics or instant healing. It's about sacred grit. About showing up when you feel unseen. About being faithful with what you have in your hands—even if what you have looks like broken pieces and tired prayers.

Rebuilding is key.

If you're reading this and you feel like your life has fallen apart—you are not disqualified. You are the rebuilder. You are the one holding the bricks. The one laying new foundations. The one God trusts with the blueprint.

And just like Nehemiah didn't rebuild alone, neither will you. God will send support. Sometimes in the form of friends. Sometimes in the form of resources. Sometimes in the still small whisper that says, "You're not done. Keep going."

You don't need perfect conditions to heal. You just need to start with what you have.

Brick by brick. Prayer by prayer.

What you are rebuilding is sacred.

Your new home. Your new boundaries. Your restored faith. Your voice.

This is your wall.

Guard it well.

Build it with grace.

And don't come down.

Live It Out Challenge | Pick Up Your Brick

Choose one sacred step—a "brick" you can lay that moves your healing forward.

Maybe it's setting a boundary, applying for a job, calling a counselor, or simply getting out of bed and trying again.

Then, choose a "sword"—a truth from scripture that will protect your peace and remind you of who you are.

In your Heart Notes, draw two columns:

- Left Column: Brick
  Write one action you'll take. A habit, a choice, a new beginning.

- Right Column: Sword
  Choose a scripture or promise to stand on this week. Example: "The joy of the Lord is your strength." —Nehemiah 8:10

Now post a guard. Who is one trusted person you can ask to pray with you, encourage you, or check in on your progress? Healing was never meant to be done alone.

Revisit Nehemiah 4:8–9.

Ask God to give you discernment—for when to build, when to rest, and when to hold the sword of truth.

Then speak this truth aloud:

"My wall is worth building. My healing is holy. And I will not come down."

Anchor Prayer | Brick by Brick

God,

I bring You what I have—these tired hands,

this trembling hope,

these pieces I'm still trying to name.

Like Nehemiah, I don't want to come down.

But I need Your strength to keep building.

Show me what brick to lay today.

Speak truth over the lies that still echo.

Help me pick up the sword of Your Word and

post a guard around my peace.

When mockers rise, steady me.

When weariness comes, hold me.

When I forget who I am, remind me:

I am Yours. I am building something sacred.

And You are not finished with me yet.

Amen.

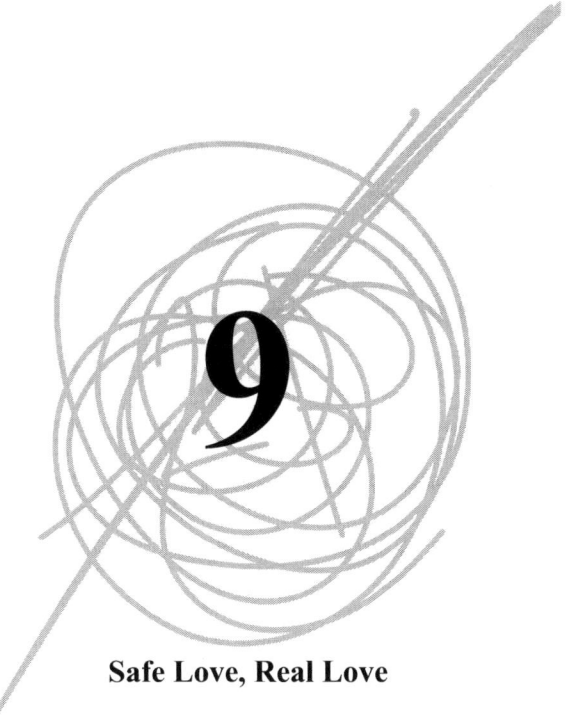

9

Safe Love, Real Love

"There is no fear in love. But perfect love drives out fear, because fear has to do with punishment. The one who fears is not made perfect in love."—1 *John 4:18*

There was a time I couldn't define love without first naming what hurt me.

If you asked me what love looked like back then, I would have said: staying. Enduring. Trying harder. Shrinking when needed. Not being "too much." Anticipating moods like weather forecasts. Cleaning everything just right. Apologizing for things I didn't do. Silencing my joy. Measuring worth by how well I kept the peace.

I believed love was earned through effort and proven by survival. That if I loved well enough, maybe the chaos would calm. Maybe the criticism would quiet. Maybe the person who praised me one day and punished me the next would eventually love me in a way that didn't hurt.

But that wasn't love.

It was fear. It was control. It was performance masquerading as partnership.

It took walking away to finally see that.

When we left, I didn't know how to feel safe in love. I didn't trust kindness. I didn't recognize healthy as safe. When someone offered a compliment, I braced for the criticism that usually followed. When someone held a door open, I wondered what it would cost me later. My nervous system had been trained to treat safety as suspicious.

Even in moments of peace, I waited for the other shoe to drop. Love had always come with conditions, with apologies, with eggshells. So when love showed up differently, I didn't know what to do with it.

Healing Love Requires Unlearning. Healing.

Learning to receive safe love after abuse is not about jumping into new relationships. It's about rebuilding the soul house that was torn down by fear. It's about retraining the heart and brain to believe that tenderness is not always a trap, that love can be both soft and safe.

And it's about starting with God.

I had to learn that love—real love—begins with the One who authored it. Think of your healing like a garden. After years of surviving on barren ground, you have to clear the rocks, pull the weeds, and tend to the soil. My soil was dry—packed down with years of unworthiness and lies. I had planted seeds before, but they never had a chance to grow.

Because abuse doesn't just crush your heart—it distorts your view of love entirely.

Love became something I had to hustle for.

But when I began to trust God again, I realized: love isn't a wage. It's a gift. It's not a performance. It's a promise.

The soil began to soften.

God began to show me that love doesn't control—it honors. Love doesn't demand—it invites. Love doesn't punish—it restores.

I used to tell myself, "It's not that bad—he's just mad. He doesn't mean to scare me." But fear was threaded into the fabric of our relationship—woven into small moments that stacked until I could no longer ignore the pattern.

One afternoon in late December, the road to our home had just been graded. Dust rose like a curtain as I turned onto the familiar stretch of dirt. That's when I saw a truck speeding toward me, straight on. The dust was so thick I could barely see. At the last second, I swerved into the ditch and slammed on the brakes—heart pounding, hands trembling.

I called, my voice shaking.

"What just happened? That could've ended badly."

The response I got was cold and dismissive:

"Next time, move."

It wasn't the first time road tension had surfaced. Not long before, there had been an incident involving a service truck on that same road—tempers flared, and things escalated. Eventually, the company removed our service altogether.

That's what control looks like when it stops pretending to be love. That's what fear sounds like when it gets disguised as protection.

It wasn't safe. And it wasn't love.

Ruth didn't chase a man. She stayed faithful to her calling, even in grief. She journeyed with Naomi not out of obligation but out of covenant. She worked in the fields—humbly, steadily—and when Boaz noticed her, it wasn't because she was loud. It was because she was steady. And when they finally united, it was not through manipulation or performance. It was through mutual honor and respect.

Esther didn't use her beauty to earn love. She used her courage to save a nation. She fasted. She prayed. She stood in the gap with trembling hands, trusting that her worth wasn't tied to whether the king accepted her. She was already chosen—by God.

Hagar, cast out and alone, met the God who sees. She wasn't rescued by a man. She was met by mercy in the wilderness. And it was God who gave her the strength to return, the eyes to see, and the legacy to hold onto.

These women didn't perform for love. They were seen. Called. Used. Loved—as they were.

So, what does that mean for us?

It means we stop striving and start receiving.

It means love can show up in safe arms, kind eyes, and no strings attached.

It means love is not measured by how many times we can endure abuse and still stay.

There was a moment—after the leaving, after the ache, after the rebuilding—when someone reached for my hand in the middle of a sentence. Just reached, gently. No words. No tension. Just presence. And I cried.

Not because of the gesture. But because I didn't flinch.

For the first time in years, my body didn't tense. My soul didn't brace. I just received it.

That was healing.

Another time, I burned dinner. Years ago, that would have been met with a rage-filled explosion. But this time? The person across the counter laughed. They opened the fridge. Made a sandwich. Kissed my forehead. We laughed, too. That was it.

No fear. No name-calling. No stonewalling.

That was love.

Safe love. Real love.

When your soul house has been torn down, you don't just need new walls. You need new wiring.

Love has to be rewired into every room. Into how you speak to yourself. How you let others speak to you. How you decorate your routines, your relationships, your rest.

I remember buying myself flowers just because. It wasn't a grand moment, but it felt revolutionary. For years, flowers had only come after abuse—an apology bouquet to cover bruises, words, wounds.

But now? I didn't need harm to earn beauty.

I gave it to myself.

That's love. 1st Corinthians 13 love.

We hear the verses at weddings. But 1 Corinthians 13 was never meant to be a ceremonial quote. It's a measuring stick for love—especially for the love we receive and the love we give.

Love is patient. Love is kind. It does not envy. It does not boast. It is not proud. It does not dishonor others. It is not self-seeking. It is not easily angered. It keeps no record of wrongs. Love does not delight in evil but rejoices with the truth. It always protects, always trusts, always hopes, always perseveres.

That's the blueprint.

That's what your soul was created to receive.

And anything less isn't love.

I didn't leap into safe love. I inched into it.

Through counseling. Through friendship. Through choosing peace when I was used to chaos. Through blessing the small moments and planting new seeds.

I let God water my soul house with mercy. I let trusted people hold space for my healing. I gave myself permission to receive without guilt.

I watched my children exhale in our new home. Watched them run free in the yard without checking to see if they were "too loud."

I watched myself exhale, too.

I laid down performance. I picked up peace.

Because that's what real love does.

It lets you rest. It lets you be. It lets you heal.

And one day, you wake up in a house you rebuilt with God, and you realize: the girl who once flinched now dances in the kitchen. The woman who once whispered now sings. The mother who once feared now prays bold, blessing-filled prayers over her babies.

Because she knows what real love feels like. And she won't settle again.

Live It Out Challenge | Rebuild Your Love Definition

In your heart notes, write a letter to yourself. Not the past you. Not the future you. But the present you.

Tell yourself what love is and declare it over every corner of your soul house!

Anchor Prayer | Loved and Seen

God,

Thank You for showing me

that love isn't something I have to earn.

Thank You for being the perfect love that casts out fear.

Help me see love through Your eyes—safe, holy, unshakable.

Teach me to live like I am already loved,

not because of what I do, but because of who You are.

Rewire the broken places. Rebuild the soul house.

Make space in me for the love You long to pour in.

Amen.

10

When the Mirror Doesn't Match the Message

"So God created mankind in His own image…" Genesis 1:27

The mirror used to lie to me—or maybe I lied to myself while staring into it. It became a battleground between who I was told I was and who God said I was. I'd look into it and see a woman warped by shame, distorted by bruises not always visible to the eye. My eyes scanned my face and body with the precision of someone hunting for flaws: the chipped tooth he caused when he threw my purse at me, the faint scar near my collarbone from the edge of a flying fan, the tightening in my jaw from years of holding back sobs.

For a long time, the mirror wasn't just glass. It was a window into my past. I could see each moment of abuse so clearly. I could feel it. I could hear it. As if it were happening.

Like the first time I felt the sting of having something thrown at me. It wasn't a slap or a punch. It was a water bottle—half full, plastic, seemingly harmless. But the message landed heavier than the object: "You are a target." From that moment, things escalated. Phones, laptops, fans, nothing was off limits. A computer screen shattered against the wall like my sense of safety. There was a time, during a heated argument about money, when my purse struck me in the face unexpectedly. I heard the crack before I felt the pain. Later, the dentist told me the damage was repairable. But how do you fix the humiliation that comes with a chipped smile?

There was never an apology for what was broke—not the furniture, not my things, not me.

Each item thrown was a declaration: "I'm bigger than you. I get to decide your worth." And little by little, I believed him. My body began to feel like an enemy. My curves, my softness, my hunger, even my reflection became suspect.

Abuse doesn't only bruise the body. It rewrites the script of worth. I started to hide in oversized clothes, not out of comfort but of punishment. I avoided mirrors or looked into them just long enough to apply makeup that masked what I didn't want to see: fatigue, fear, emptiness.

There's a peculiar kind of betrayal when your body becomes the battlefield for someone else's war.

When I was told I was "too much"—too emotional, too big, too needy—I started shrinking in every way that mattered. I stopped eating meals and started picking at food. I stopped walking tall and began slouching to avoid attention. I disconnected from my own skin.

And the mirror became proof. I wasn't enough. Or I was too much. Either way, I was wrong.

But then came grace. Quiet. Persistent. Holy.

One morning, after a particularly brutal night when he had shattered a fan in our barn and stormed out, I stood in front of the bathroom mirror and whispered, "God, show me what You see."

Tears blurred my vision, but I didn't look away. And slowly—almost imperceptibly at first—I saw something new. Not the chipped tooth or the tired eyes. Not the body shaped by stress and survival.

I saw a woman still standing.

Still breathing.

Still worthy.

Genesis 1:27 echoed like a balm to my soul: "So God created mankind in His own image…" I wasn't an accident. I wasn't broken merchandise on clearance. I was made in the image of a creative, loving, powerful God. And that made everything different.

Relearning how to see yourself is sacred work. Healing doesn't always show up in big declarations or dramatic makeovers. Sometimes it looks like standing naked in front of a mirror and saying, "Thank you, God, for this body that carried me through hell."

Sometimes it's choosing to eat, not because you feel thin enough to deserve a meal, but because you are alive and nourishment is holy.

Other times, healing looks like smiling with that chipped tooth and declaring it a badge of survival—not shame.

It took time, but I started blessing my mirror.

Literally.

Every week, I used a dry-erase marker to write truths I needed to believe: "You are fearfully and wonderfully made." "You are not the damage done to you." "You are seen and deeply loved."

At first, I said them out of obedience. But somewhere between whispering those words and living them, I started to believe.

There's a Japanese art form called kintsugi, where broken pottery is repaired with gold. Instead of hiding the cracks, it highlights them, making the vessel even more beautiful. That's what God does with us. He doesn't throw us away because of broken pieces. He fills those cracks with grace and calls them beautiful.

My chipped tooth? Fixed. But I'll never forget how I got it. Not because I want to relive the pain, but because I want to remember the strength it took to survive—and the God who never once turned away from the wreckage.

My stretch marks? They're love notes from the body that carried my child, that grew life even when I felt like I was dying inside.

My arms? Strong enough now to carry groceries, hold my boys, hug friends, and raise in worship.

My body is no longer a prison. It's a temple. A living, breathing, sacred dwelling for the Spirit of God.

If you've ever flinched at your reflection, I see you. If you've avoided mirrors, torn up old pictures, or felt like your worth was tied to your weight, your shape, your skin—hear me now:

You are not your size.

You are not the things he threw.

You are not the names you were called.

You are not the absence of affirmation.

You are not what society says you should be.

You are what God says you are—beloved, chosen, beautiful, whole.

One afternoon, I caught myself smiling in the mirror—not checking for flaws or wondering what he'd say. Just smiling. Not because I'd reached a goal weight. Not because someone complimented me.

But because I was starting to believe the truth I wrote on that mirror: "You are enough because God made you."

That was the day I realized I didn't need the world's permission to feel beautiful.

That was the day I forgave my body for all the years I thought it had failed me.

That was the day I chose to love myself—not because I was healed, but because I was healing.

Your mirror may still feel like a battlefield. That's okay. Start there.

Bring your shame, your silence, your stories.

Then speak life into it.

Name your truth. Write it down. Bless the very place where lies used to linger.

You don't have to wait until you "feel" confident to practice truth.

Healing happens in motion. In repetition. In resistance to the lie.

You are not broken beyond repair.

You are becoming.

You are already beloved.

Love Big Challenge | Bless the Mirror

Pick one sacred step that helps you reclaim how you see yourself.

Think small. Think holy. Think brave.

- Maybe it's standing in front of the mirror for five seconds longer than yesterday—even if your heart races.
- Maybe it's looking past the chipped tooth, the scar, the curve you once called shame—and whispering "thank you" instead of critique.
- Maybe it's throwing away the baggy sweatshirt you used to hide in, or replacing it with something that makes you feel alive.
- Maybe it's writing I am still standing in dry-erase marker on your mirror because that's all you can say today.

Whatever it is, name it. This is your brick. This is one act that declares:

"I'm not who he said I was. I'm building something new."

Anchor Prayer | Mirror by Mirror

God,

You saw me when the mirror only showed damage.

You stayed when I covered myself in shame and silence.

You wept when he threw my purse and shattered my smile.

You called me beautiful before I ever dared to believe it.

Help me bless what I once belittled.

Help me stand still and see—the strength it took to survive.

Help me write truth on my mirror and speak it into my skin.

When the old voices rise, arm me with Your Word.

When I avoid the mirror, whisper: "Look again, daughter."

When I feel too much, too broken, too scarred—remind me:

I am Yours.

I am whole.

And I am worth seeing.

Amen.

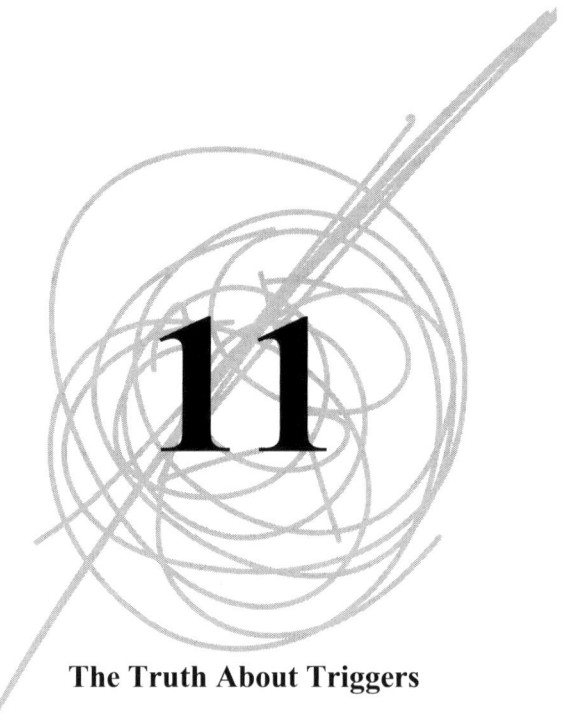

The Truth About Triggers

"When the righteous cry for help, the Lord hears and delivers them out of all their troubles."—Psalm 34:17

In the language of Scripture, a trigger is not explicitly named as we understand it today—but the Bible overflows with stories of people whose souls were stirred by grief, fear, shame, or the echo of past wounds. Think of David, who trembled in caves after Saul's threats. Or Elijah, who fled in despair after victory. What we now call "triggers," Scripture often frames as deep soul responses to past harm or trauma— emotional echoes that impact present decisions.

A trigger, in biblical terms, is a signpost pointing to a wound that still needs tending. It's the place where God often whispers, "I see you there." Rather than dismissing those reactions, the Bible shows us that God moves toward us in our most vulnerable moments. Psalm 147:3 says, "He heals the brokenhearted and binds up their wounds." That means your reaction isn't weakness—it's an invitation for healing.

And what about truth? According to John 8:32, "Then you will know the truth, and the truth will set you free." Truth in the Bible is not just information. It is a Person—Jesus. And it's a balm. Truth is what dismantles lies. It's the light that chases away the shadow. Truth tells us who we are and whose we are—even when triggers try to tell a different story.

The Bible teaches that truth does not change based on our feelings or fears. Truth stands firm, like a rock in the storm. Proverbs 30:5 says, "Every word of God proves true; he is a shield to those who take refuge in him." In other words, when triggers shout lies at us, God's truth speaks louder—if we let it.

So, in this chapter, we're going to explore what it looks like to live with triggers through the lens of God's truth. To stop being afraid of the reaction and instead begin asking: what is this showing me? What can I heal here? Where is God meeting me in this?

Because triggers, while painful, are also places of potential transformation.

There are moments I still walk into a room and freeze—no visible danger, no clear threat, but my body remembers. That's what a trigger does. It bypasses logic and grabs you by the gut. It tells you the past is present, even when you know better. It pulls fear to the surface like a ghost.

For me, triggers weren't always big, dramatic moments. Sometimes, it was the most ordinary things: walking into a hotel lobby that smelled like the place we stayed during one of his rage-filled business trips. Hearing a certain song from a concert we went to, the one where he stormed out because I didn't laugh at the right time. Seeing a white pickup truck that looked just like his.

Other times, they hit like a wave I didn't see coming. Like the first time I walked into a livestock barn after we left. I was just trying to support my boys. But the scent of hay, the buzz of the fans, the shuffle of boots on concrete—all of it collapsed onto me like a weight. It was as if my lungs forgot how to work. I had to walk outside and count my breaths, tell myself I was safe.

Even pictures became landmines. I found an old image of us once—me smiling, at a stock show, we looked seemingly content. I looked so happy. But the memory behind the photo? It was taken after one of his worst outbursts. The hotel room had been destroyed the night before. We had faked the moment for the camera. My smile wasn't joy. It was survival.

There's one moment that still lingers in my memory like heavy air: I was standing in the garage, barefoot and exhausted. Tension escalated after a comment I made. In the chaos, a trash can was suddenly thrown in my direction. As I reached to block it, a sharp edge caught my hand—deep enough to require stitches. I stood there in stunned silence, holding my bleeding hand, trying to make sense of what had just happened. When I asked why, there was no apology—just a dismissive comment that left a deeper mark than the wound itself.

That was the pattern. Phones. Water bottles. Laptops. Lamps. Anything within reach became a weapon of control. The flying object was never the point. The point was to make me afraid. To make me question if I was safe enough to speak.

Triggers are cruel that way. They don't wait for permission. They don't care if you've "moved on." They come uninvited, asking for attention you don't want to give. And yet, they become some of the most sacred invitations in our healing—not to relive the trauma, but to rewrite the story.

That's what God started to show me: the trigger wasn't proof I was broken. It was proof I had survived. That my body still remembered what my soul had endured—and that God was near, even in the panic.

And that's where the woman from the Bible I think of often comes in: Mary Magdalene.

We met her earlier in this book, and now she returns as a witness to what healing can look like on the other side of trauma.

Mary knew what it meant to be haunted—seven demons once lived inside her. Seven. That's not just spiritual possession; that's a life consumed. A soul tormented. And yet, Jesus met her in that place and set her free.

But what I find most profound is what came next: Mary followed Him. She didn't shrink back. She stayed. Even when things got hard. Even when trauma reared its head again—like at the crucifixion, when she stood near the cross, watching the One who saved her suffer.

Can you imagine the triggers in that moment? The sounds of weeping. The smell of blood and sweat. The crowd shouting insults. The chaos. And still, she stayed. Her love kept her grounded. Her healing didn't remove all pain—but it gave her strength to face it.

And she was the first one to see the resurrected Christ.

That's what rewriting looks like.

The very places where pain once lived become holy ground.

A trigger, once acknowledged and paired with truth, loses some of its power. The more often we recognize it, speak truth to it, and walk through it rather than around it—the more our brains rewire toward healing. Every time you feel a trigger and respond differently—with prayer, with grounding, with compassion—you're not failing. You're forming new pathways of trust and safety.

When we repeatedly interrupt a trigger with truth, our nervous system slowly begins to reprogram itself. The brain learns that the danger has passed. The body starts to unlearn panic. Over time, what used to hijack your day becomes a moment of connection with God instead—a sacred pause rather than a full-body spiral.

You begin to recognize the difference between trauma and truth—not because the memories disappear, but because you've rewritten your response. That's healing. That's holy. That's the power of pairing God's Word with our wounds.

You do not have to stay stuck in the loop of fear. Healing is possible. Not perfect healing, but faithful healing. And the more often you choose truth, the more familiar that truth becomes. One moment, one breath, one prayer at a time.

God is not ashamed of your triggers. He meets you in them.

He is doing the holy work of reclaiming your nervous system with peace one courageous moment at a time.

Let Him walk with you through each one.

Live It Out Challenge | Trace the Trigger

Reflect on one trigger in your Heart Notes—just one. Name it. Write the story it tells you. Then, rewrite that story through the lens of God's truth. Use Psalm 94:19 as your anchor: "When anxiety was great within me, your consolation brought me joy."

- What does this trigger tell you about your past?
- What does it try to convince you of now?
- What does God say instead?

Write it out.

Speak it aloud.

Tell someone you trust.

You are not crazy.

You are healing.

You are not alone.

You are seen.

Your body is not betraying you.

It's inviting you to deeper healing.

And you, brave one, are safe to heal here.

Anchor Prayer | Rewrite My Reaction

God,

Thank You for never leaving me in the panic.

When my heart races and my breath shortens,

remind me that You are near.

Help me trace the roots of my fear, not to stay there, but

to rewrite them with Your truth.

Where I feel afraid, speak peace.

Where I feel weak, be my strength.

Where I feel unseen, remind me that You are the God who sees.

Thank You for loving me even in the triggered moments.

Rewire my nervous system with grace.

Restore my mind with truth.

And help me heal in layers, one brave breath at a time.

Amen.

12

Grief, Grace, and Growth

"You keep track of all my sorrows. You have collected all my tears in your bottle. You have recorded each one in your book." —Psalm 56:8

There is a sacred moment in every survivor's story where the pain and the power collide. For me, it happened the night I walked away. I didn't leave with a suitcase of clarity. I didn't leave with applause or a five-step plan for healing. I left with a bleeding heart, shaking hands, and a soul full of silent prayers. But I walked away knowing this: I would never be abused again.

That was the moment I claimed victory. Not over a man. Not even over my past. But over the idea that I was powerless to change it. In that space, trembling and unsure, I chose myself. I chose freedom. I chose God. And I chose to believe that even grief could be a beginning.

What they don't tell you about healing is that it comes with grief. Not just the grief of what was done to you, but the grief of everything you lost along the way. The time. The identity. The girl you used to be. The dreams you deferred. The birthdays you faked a smile through. The innocence that was chipped away with every slammed door, every insult disguised as a joke, every apology that came with conditions.

Grief shows up in the quiet hours when your body still braces for an outburst. It lingers in the grocery store aisle where you used to rush through with anxiety. It breathes down your neck at family gatherings, when no one mentions what you left, but the tension is loud anyway. It walks beside you when your child asks a question you can't fully answer yet. It curls up in bed with you when you're trying to sleep but your heart is still on high alert.

And yet, grief isn't the enemy. It's the evidence of love. The price of survival. The echo of what you were brave enough to walk through. It deserves space, not shame. You do not have to choose between grieving and growing. You can hold both in the same breath. And you must.

I remember the first time I let myself cry after leaving. Not the stifled, hidden tears that slipped out when no one was looking. I mean the full-body, breath-stealing sobs that gutted me to my core. I was sitting in my car in a gas station parking lot, holding a soda I didn't even want, staring at the sunset through a cracked windshield. I cried for everything—for what I had survived, for what my children had witnessed, for the way I had learned to minimize my own pain just to keep the peace.

And somewhere in that cry, I felt God whisper, I saw it all.

Every silent tear. Every slammed door. Every moment I shrank just to stay safe. He had collected every one of my tears. None of them were wasted. None of them forgotten. Psalm 56:8 became my anchor in those days: "You have collected all my tears in your bottle."

Grief wasn't a detour from healing. It was the doorway. It wasn't weakness. It was worship—the kind that comes when you finally feel safe enough to fall apart.

Letting myself grieve meant honoring the woman I was in those years of survival. She was exhausted, yes. But she was also resilient. She got out of bed when it felt impossible. She wore sunglasses to hide the circles under her eyes. She prayed while folding laundry. She covered bruises with makeup and excuses. She made dinner with a lump in her throat and still kissed foreheads goodnight. She took the insults and the threats and still whispered affirmations under her breath.

She was not weak. She was divine strength in skin and bones. And I needed to thank her.

That version of me carried us through.

So, I began to practice what I now call holy gratitude. Not for the abuse. Never that. But for the grit that grew in the darkness. For the faith that survived the silence. For the strength I didn't know I had until I saw what I walked through.

I lit candles. I wrote letters to the woman I was. I started each one the same way: Thank you for surviving.

Grace came next. And let me be clear: grace isn't always soft. Sometimes it feels like fire. Sometimes it confronts. Grace meant I had to stop blaming myself for the years I stayed. It meant releasing the shame of how long it took me to leave. Grace meant not having the answers and choosing healing anyway.

Grace reminded me that God wasn't ashamed of my timeline. He wasn't waiting for a polished version of me. He was present in the mess, in the middle, in the mourning. He wasn't rushing me through grief. He was walking me through it.

I remember reading Isaiah 61:3 one night: "...to bestow on them a crown of beauty instead of ashes, the oil of joy instead of mourning, and a garment of praise instead of a spirit of despair."

It hit me like a promise. That one day, my mourning would make way for joy. Not a fake smile or a forced hope. But a deep, holy kind of joy that could only be born through the fire.

Growth showed up slowly. Quietly. In the little things. The first time I laughed without looking over my shoulder. The first time I bought flowers for myself. The first night I slept through without dreams of running or hiding.

Growth looked like setting boundaries and not apologizing. It looked like saying "no" without explanation. It looked like letting people love me without suspicion. It looked like showing up to church and not feeling like I was too broken to belong. It looked like watching my boys laugh freely and knowing the sound wasn't laced with fear.

Growth wasn't linear. It came with setbacks. With tears in therapy. With waves of guilt and unexpected grief. But it came. It came when I let grief lead me to grace, and grace lead me to growth.

And on the other side of it, I found something I never expected:

Peace.

Not perfection.

Not a life without hard things.

But peace rooted in the fact that I had come through the fire, and I was still standing.

If you are grieving today, let me say this: You are allowed to mourn what happened. You are allowed to miss the good moments, even in the middle of the bad. You are allowed to cry for the woman who didn't know yet. You are allowed to feel it all.

Grief does not disqualify you from healing. It prepares you for it.

Let grace catch you there.

And let that grace become your fuel. Not the kind that pushes you to fake it, but the kind that lifts your chin and says, we're going to make it.

You don't have to prove anything. You just have to keep breathing. Keep honoring the woman you were. Keep letting God rewrite what shame tried to ruin.

Live It Out Challenge | Light a Candle for Her

Take some quiet time this week to honor the version of you that survived.

Light a candle in her name. Then, write her a letter.

Start with these words:

Dear brave one,

Thank her. Speak life over her. Tell her what you see now that she couldn't. Tell her she was never weak. That her survival was sacred. That her voice still matters.

And then, declare one thing you are grateful to her for. Say it aloud. Write it somewhere visible.

Let that candle be a symbol. Of grief. Of grace. Of growth. Of all the ways you are still becoming.

Anchor Prayer | Sacred Tears

God,

Thank You for collecting every one of my tears.

Thank You for sitting with me in the grief and

not rushing me through it.

Thank You for grace that meets me where I am and

grows me gently.

Help me honor the woman I was.

Help me see her not with shame, but with sacred compassion.

Where sorrow lingers, bring comfort.

Where regret lives, bring release.

Where fear remains, bring peace.

Thank You for turning ashes into beauty.

And for walking with me, every step of the way.

Amen.

Love That Leads You Home

"The rain came down, the streams rose, and the winds blew and beat against that house; yet it did not fall, because it had its foundation on the rock." —Matthew 7:25

Some moments shift everything—not because they erase the past, but because they finally give you permission to grieve it.

For us, that moment came when we got the call that our belongings—what remained of them—could be picked up. After months of not knowing where our things had gone, of sleeping on borrowed beds and living out of bins, we were given back what had been taken. But it didn't come tied with a neat bow. Most of it was broken, taken apart screw by screw, laid out in pieces like some kind of cruel metaphor for what we'd lived through.

And yet, it was ours. It was what was left. It was what we had survived for.

We took it home—not back to where the pain lived, but forward into something new. Into a house we bought. It was perfect and it was completely ours. We closed on it with trembling hands and tear-filled eyes. Not because it was big. Not because it was fancy. But because it was a promise fulfilled. A sacred exhale. A physical reminder that God is in the rebuilding business.

This house became more than a roof—it became the canvas of our healing.

We didn't just hang curtains—we created emotional safety. We didn't just put together furniture—we pieced together peace. Each room we blessed was a declaration: we are not going back. We are loved. We are safe. We are whole.

For the first time in years, we were no longer guests in someone else's space. We could walk barefoot. We could sing loud. We could leave dishes in the sink and not fear the consequence. The door didn't slam in rage—it closed softly with grace.

God had not only delivered us from abuse—He led us to restoration. Buying that house was a holy marker. Not because it fixed everything— but because it marked the shift from surviving to truly living. It marked the shift from just making it through to making something new. It gave us space to grieve what had been stolen—and celebrate what we were building.

We cried over boxes of broken things. But we also danced in the kitchen. We mourned over photos bent by water damage. But we laughed under new blankets and new light. This was sacred ground.

Because love—real love—leads us home. First, to the heart of God. Then, to ourselves. And finally, to the physical and emotional places where healing grows.

God does this again and again in Scripture. He leads His people out of bondage and into belonging. He calls them out of slavery and into the Promised Land. He takes what's been scattered and brings it back together.

That's what He did for us.

We didn't just move into a house. We were moved by the love of a God who saw us—who fought for us, who gave us strength to keep building even when it felt like we had nothing left.

There's a sacred shift that happens when the weight of survival begins to lift, and the weight of presence settles in. When you no longer have to brace for impact. When you can actually breathe deeply—not just out of necessity, but as worship.

That house, those walls, those rooms—they became sacred spaces where we unlearned fear. Where we began to trust joy again. Where healing came not in one sweeping cinematic moment, but in small, sacred choices. A new bedtime routine. A dinner with laughter. A prayer whispered at the sink.

Even grief felt different in our home. It had space. It could sit beside us without taking over the whole room. We gave it permission to exist, but we also gave it boundaries.

We could finally grieve being homeless—not in a technical sense, but in a spiritual and emotional one. Grieve what it felt like to live without safety, without rest, without roots. And in that grief, we also praised. We celebrated what had returned. What had been resurrected. What we had been given.

And isn't that the invitation of God? Not just to survive the wilderness, but to make a home in the Promised Land.

Home, in the spiritual sense, isn't just where you live. It's where you return to yourself. It's where you reconnect with God's voice. It's where you feel seen, known, and safe.

In Scripture, building a home was sacred. It meant permanence. Safety. Identity. The Israelites were told to build their homes and plant gardens in the land where God placed them (Jeremiah 29:5). To establish roots. To believe in a future even in unfamiliar places. God gave instructions for building homes not just to provide shelter, but to remind His people of belonging.

Proverbs 24:3–4 tells us, "By wisdom a house is built, and through understanding it is established; through knowledge its rooms are filled with rare and beautiful treasures." This is what home became for us. Not just walls and windows, but wisdom. Not just furniture, but understanding. Not just routines, but rare and beautiful treasures of trust, peace, and love.

Our house became that. But so did our hearts.

I began to trust again. Myself. My kids. My God.

I began to rebuild not just routines, but rhythms: Friday movies. Sunday quiet time. Meals on the patio. Worship music in the mornings. Laughter without apology.

I began to know myself not by what had happened to me, but by what I was becoming. And the boys? They began to glow. To settle. To root themselves in the safety we had prayed for and fought for.

It didn't matter that most of what we got back was damaged. That furniture had been dismantled. That pieces were missing.

Because God gave us what we needed: the pieces that still mattered. The pieces that told the story of our survival. The ones worth reassembling.

Piece by piece, we put our lives back together.

Not everything fit the way it used to. That's part of healing. Some things stay in boxes. Some you let go. Some you repurpose into something new. But all of it—every chipped plate, every bent photo frame—became part of the holy mosaic of our new life.

A life built not in fear, but in freedom.

A home anchored not by perfection, but by peace.

So if you're still waiting for your house, your healing, your home—I hope this chapter is proof that it's possible.

And when it comes, you'll know.

Because love—God's love—will lead you there.

Live It Out Challenge | Build a Sacred Home

This week, choose one corner of your world to become a sacred space. It doesn't have to be a house. It can be a chair, a journal, a playlist, a prayer room. Wherever your soul feels at home.

Add something that reminds you who you are and whose you are:

- A scripture
- A candle
- A song
- A photo that represents healing
- A note of encouragement from someone who sees you

Let this space be a physical reminder that love leads you here.

You don't have to earn it. You don't have to strive for it. You just have to receive it.

Because God's love doesn't just restore what was lost. It rebuilds what's next.

Anchor Prayer | Love Me Home

God,

You are my refuge and my restoration.

Thank You for bringing me through the dark into light.

Thank You for every step of healing, every corner of grace.

Help me build a life that reflects Your goodness.

Help me create a home—within and around me—

where love lives and peace reigns.

May this space, however simple, be holy ground.

May this new season be full of laughter, healing, and truth.

Lead me home, again and again, into Your heart.

And help me remember:

I am safe here.

I am seen here.

I am loved here.

Amen.

14

Redeeming the Middle

"Thus far the Lord has helped us." —1 Samuel 7:12

There's something holy about the middle.

We don't talk about it much. We love a good beginning—full of hope, fresh starts, and possibility. We love the endings, too—the victory lap, the closure, the final bow. But the middle? It's murky. It's the season where the dust hasn't quite settled and the miracle hasn't yet arrived. It's the Tuesday of healing. The valley between the mountaintops. The comma in the sentence that hasn't ended yet.

And yet, the middle is where most of us spend our lives.

The middle is laundry and paperwork. Appointments and events. It's waking up in a bed that you finally feel safe in but still battling the nightmares that try to pull you back. It's both gratitude and grief tangled up in the same breath.

In the middle, the wounds aren't fresh, but they're not fully healed either. You've walked away from the chaos, but you haven't quite walked into the clarity. You're no longer in survival mode, but you haven't reached full restoration.

You're somewhere in between.

And that is holy ground.

Because it's in the middle that your faith gets legs. It's in the middle that you choose to keep going, even when the finish line is still out of sight. It's in the middle that you look around and realize: you're still here.

In Scripture, there's a moment that marks this beautifully.

In 1 Samuel 7, after a season of war and repentance, the prophet Samuel sets up a stone and calls it "Ebenezer," which means "stone of help." He says, "Thus far the Lord has helped us."

It wasn't the beginning of their story. It wasn't the end. It was the middle. And Samuel chose to mark it. To pause. To name the faithfulness of God in the in-between.

Throughout Scripture, stones are used to mark moments of meaning. Jacob used a stone as a pillow in the wilderness—waking from a dream of heaven and naming that place Bethel, the house of God. Joshua commanded the Israelites to carry stones out of the Jordan as a sign of God's faithfulness in bringing them across. Jesus Himself is called the Cornerstone. Each stone marked movement, presence, promise.

What if we did that too?

What if we stopped rushing through the middle and started redeeming it? There was a season when I thought healing meant getting to the end of the pain. I thought there would be a day when it all just clicked into place. But that day never came in the way I expected.

Instead, what came were small victories in the middle:

- The first time I laughed and didn't feel guilty.
- The day I sat through church without tears rolling down my cheeks.
- The moment my son called our house "home."

These weren't the end of the story. But they were markers. Ebenezers. Stones of help.

And they mattered.

In the Bible, stones marked passages—crossings. The middle of something hard becoming something holy. Maybe your stack of stones looks like sticky notes on your mirror. Maybe it's the email you finally sent. The boundary you finally set. The dinner you cooked after weeks of frozen meals.

Maybe your middle is messy.

But maybe it's also miraculous.

One of the most powerful declarations in the middle is this: I'm still here. Still breathing. Still hoping. Still trying. Still believing.

Still showing up when it would be easier to disappear.

There's nothing glamorous about the middle. It's not filled with applause. There's no highlight reel. But there is substance. There is soul work. There is holy grit.

In the middle, I learned how to be kind to myself. I stopped measuring my worth by my productivity. I started listening to my body. I drank water. I prayed short, breathy prayers. I let the laundry pile up so I could play Uno with my kids. I went to counseling. I said "no" more often. I cried in the car and then wiped my face and kept going.

And through it all, God never left.

God is not only the God of our breakthroughs—He is the God of our between seasons. Of our waiting. Of our questions. Of our slow, steady, ordinary days.

The middle is the between.

The middle is not wasted. It's where the roots grow.

Think of a seed. It's planted in the dark. Buried. Hidden. It doesn't look like life is happening. But underground, everything is changing. The seed is breaking open, pushing through, reaching for the surface.

That's what healing feels like. That's what the middle does. It prepares you for the bloom.

God doesn't despise your middle. He meets you in it.

Think of Ruth, gleaning in the fields—quiet, humble faithfulness after loss. Think of Esther, fasting and waiting—caught between a past she couldn't return to and a future that hadn't yet revealed itself. Think of Hagar, in the wilderness—desperate, alone, and yet met by a God who sees.

Their stories didn't hinge on glamorous beginnings or neat endings. Their stories were forged in the middle—in the waiting, in the weeping, in the choosing to believe that God still sees them.

He sees you, too.

Right here. Right now. In the not-quite-there.

The middle is also where the harvest begins. Where the seed dies and something new sprouts up. Jesus referenced the middle often. The middle of storms. The middle of crowds. The middle of suffering. It's where transformation is born.

Imagine a world with no middle—just a beginning and an end. We would miss the lessons. The growth. The resilience. The intimacy with God that's forged in fire, not ease. Without the middle, we would lose our becoming.

Imagine the story of Esther without her time in the palace waiting and praying. Or Ruth without the days in the field, gathering behind harvesters. The waiting was where their trust grew deep, and their character was formed. The middle was the hinge between the heartbreak and the healing. It's the long inhale before the miracle.

What if the middle is the place where God is forming you into who you need to be for what's next? What if the middle isn't punishment—but preparation?

The middle teaches us to live present. To find God not just in breakthroughs, but in the breath between them. It teaches us to look around and say, "Even here, even now, God is good."

That kind of faith—that middle faith—is the stuff that builds legacies. This chapter is your permission slip to stop striving for the end and start standing in the middle with purpose.

It's a reminder that your progress is holy. That your partial healing is still healing. That your wobbly steps are still forward motion.

So today, mark your middle.

Write it down. Say it out loud. Stack a stone. Light a candle. Make a playlist.

Do something that reminds you: you're still here.

And that matters.

Choose one milestone from your current season. It could be something big—like a new job, a healing breakthrough, or walking away from something painful—or something quiet and unseen, like getting out of bed when you didn't want to, setting a boundary, or telling the truth out loud.

Write a declaration that begins with:

✦ *"I'm still here because..."*

Be honest. Be bold. Be tender with yourself.

Maybe you're still here because God held you when no one else knew how.
Maybe you're still here because you chose courage over comfort.
Maybe you're still here because the story isn't over—and deep down, you know it.

Next, place your declaration somewhere visible:

- On your mirror
- Inside your journal
- As your phone background
- On your car dash
- Beside your coffee pot

Anchor Prayer | Still Here, Still Held

God,

Thank You for meeting me in the middle.

For the moments no one else sees.

For the breath I still have.

For the progress I've made.

Remind me that this in-between space is not empty.

It's full of Your presence.

I don't have to rush to the end.

I don't have to fear what's ahead.

I just have to keep walking—with You.

Thank You for holding me steady.

Thank You for loving me right here.

Amen.

Forgiveness that Frees You

"Be kind and compassionate to one another, forgiving each other, just as in Christ God forgave you." —Ephesians 4:32

There's a reason bitterness is compared to poison—not because it looks deadly, but because it slowly becomes deadly. A silent seep. A slow rot. It's bitter not in taste, but in impact. It curdles joy. It erodes peace. It stains every good thing with the shadow of what was done to you. And it's heavy.

That's the thing about unforgiveness—it becomes a weight we weren't designed to carry. It tells you it's protecting you, when really, it's imprisoning you. It whispers, "You'll be weak if you let this go." But what it really does is shackle your soul to the pain of what happened. And when you stay tethered to that pain, you can't walk freely into the future God has for you.

Forgiveness, then, is not just a kindness you extend—it is a key you hand yourself. It's the holy release that makes room for healing.

Before you can move forward, you must unburden your heart.

The abuse was not your fault.

Say that again—out loud if you need to.

The abuse was not your fault.

You didn't cause it. You didn't deserve it. And you were never meant to carry it. That burden belongs to the one who did the harm—not the one who survived it. And yet, we carry it anyway. In clenched fists and sleepless nights. In guarded relationships and second-guessing our instincts. In the way we flinch at kindness or build walls around our hearts like they're fortresses.

But what if that weight isn't your protection? What if it's your prison? When you carry the burden of abuse, it presses down on every part of your being. It echoes in your mind, disrupts your breath, taints your joy. It's like trying to build a home on a foundation of rubble. Every truth you try to plant gets choked out by the debris of the past. Every seed of joy you water gets suffocated under the weight of resentment.

It doesn't just limit your peace—it limits your purpose.

You cannot run your race while dragging chains.

To understand forgiveness, you must also understand what it is not.

Let's be clear: forgiveness is not reconciliation. It's not forgetting. It's not excusing. It's not pretending it didn't happen. It's not welcoming someone back into your life who is still unsafe.

Forgiveness is releasing what is not yours to carry.

It's setting the prisoner free—and realizing the prisoner was you.

Forgiveness doesn't mean what they did was okay. It means you are okay. Okay enough to lay it down. Okay enough to say, "This happened, but it does not define me." Okay enough to step forward—not because they deserve it, but because you deserve peace. You deserve freedom. You deserve space to breathe and joy that's not punctuated by flashbacks.

So what happens when we don't forgive?

Imagine dragging a heavy sack filled with bricks labeled:

- "What they said."
- "What they did."
- "What I lost."
- "Who I used to be."

Every step forward becomes harder.

You try to garden joy, but the soil is dry. The weeds of resentment overtake your soul house. The walls start to crumble. Not because God isn't present—but because the foundation is crowded. There is no room for peace when bitterness is the tenant.

You were created to flourish. But when bitterness is rooted in your heart, it stunts every beautiful thing that wants to grow. You find yourself asking, "Why don't I feel happy?" "Why can't I trust?" "Why do I keep circling back to this pain?"

It's because your heart is still carrying something toxic.

Bitterness rewrites the narrative. It convinces you that your identity is tied to what happened to you instead of who God says you are. It lies. And forgiveness is how you tell the truth.

Jesus carried the ultimate burden of injustice.

Mocked. Betrayed. Beaten. Nailed to a cross.

And from that place of agony, He said, "Father, forgive them."

He released what was not His to carry so that we could be free.

If Jesus, the most innocent person to ever walk this earth, could forgive those who hurt Him—then forgiveness is not about merit. It's about mercy.

Forgiveness is not earned. It is given.

Not always to them—but always to you.

Because when you forgive, you step out of the role of victim and into the posture of victory. You release what poisons your peace so that you can finally breathe again.

God's Word says in Colossians 3:13, "Bear with each other and forgive one another… Forgive as the Lord forgave you." The call to forgive is not to forget the pain but to refuse to be chained to it.

I've had to forgive in layers.

It didn't happen all at once. It happened in grocery aisles, phone calls, hallways, in the middle of the night when I replayed the worst of it and whispered, "God, take this. I don't want to carry it anymore."

I've had to forgive when I was triggered. When I saw his truck. When I heard the rumors. When I sat at my son's football game and saw people cheer for someone who broke me.

I had to forgive the silence. The people who knew but said nothing. The ones who judged from a distance without ever hearing my side.

I even had to forgive myself. For staying too long. For trying too hard. For believing the lies. For bending to the point of breaking.

Forgiveness became my protest. Forgiveness became my freedom song.

Not because the pain was erased—but because I chose not to be defined by it.

What does it mean to live free?

Forgiveness clears the clutter. It lets the light back in. It creates holy space in your soul house for joy, peace, and truth to take root again.

The freedom that comes with forgiveness is not fragile. It's fierce. It's the kind of strength that builds new futures. The kind of strength that makes room for new dreams.

Living free means you're no longer defined by your pain. It means your decisions are made in peace, not in fear. It means your joy doesn't apologize for existing.

You laugh louder. You breathe deeper. You sleep through the night. You walk through your life with your head high—not because you haven't been broken, but because you've been made whole.

So, what does God say about this release?

God never asked you to carry what He already died to set you free from. Isaiah 61:1 tells us that Jesus came "to bind up the brokenhearted, to proclaim freedom for the captives and release from darkness for the prisoners."

That means your healing is part of His mission. Your forgiveness is a sacred act of obedience that aligns you with Heaven's plan for your life. To release the weight is to say: "God, I trust You more than I trust my pain."

When you let go of bitterness, you make room for grace. When you release the anger, you create space for joy. When you lay down the burden, you stand up taller in your calling.

This truth remains: You were not made to carry this.

The abuse was real. The harm was deep. The cost was great.

But the burden is not yours.

It was never meant to be yours.

Lay it down at the feet of Jesus. Leave it there. And walk forward—lighter, freer, unbound.

Love Big Challenge | Release the Weight
What you carry shapes how you move.

But some of what you're holding—anger, disappointment, betrayal, shame—was never yours to keep. It may have protected you for a season, but it's time to let it go.

Step 1: Name the Weight
Write down one resentment, hurt, or heavy feeling you're still holding.
Use scrap paper. Be honest. Be real.

Step 2: Pray Over It
Hold the paper and say a short prayer:

"God, I give this to You. Help me let it go."

Step 3: Let It Go
Tear it. Burn it. Shred it.
Whatever feels right—just release it.

Step 4: Say This Out Loud

"I release what is not mine to carry."

Let that be your turning point.
You are not stuck. You are not a hostage.
You are free.

Anchor Prayer | Set Free, Still Whole

God,

I've carried this weight for far too long.

It's broken my peace, dimmed my joy, and clouded my path.

But today, I lay it down.

Not because they deserve it—but because I do.

I release what is not mine to carry.

I release the bitterness, the blame, the resentment, the rage.

Fill the empty places with Your peace.

Water the soil of my heart.

Let forgiveness grow where fear once lived.

Let freedom rise where hurt once lingered.

I'm ready to be whole.

I'm ready to be free.

I'm ready to live.

Amen.

16

Becoming the Breakthrough

"When you walk through the fire, you shall not be burned, and the flame shall not consume you." —Isaiah 43:2

The day I walked into the courthouse, my knees shook beneath my dress. I could feel my pulse in my throat, each step heavier than the last. My chest was tight, like a hundred invisible hands were pressing down, trying to stop me from breathing—trying to stop me from going through with it.

I was facing my greatest fear.

Him.

The one who once held my heart and crushed it in secret. The one who wore charm like a mask and cruelty like a second skin. The one who told me I'd never survive without him.

I wanted to disappear. My body betrayed me with trembling hands and tear-stained makeup I kept trying to fix in the rearview mirror. But I walked in anyway—every step defiant, every inhale a silent prayer.

I didn't walk in like a warrior. I walked in wounded. But even in that moment, I felt it—the faint whisper of heaven reminding me: Courage isn't the absence of fear. It's the decision to move forward anyway.

The fluorescent lights buzzed overhead, but it was the silence in my spirit that screamed the loudest. I remembered the rooms where we used to laugh. The patio where he once promised forever. Now I was showing up for me—for freedom. For peace. For my future.

No one clapped. No one knew what it took to show up that day. But heaven saw. God saw. And I felt Him with me—not after the gavel fell, but right there in the ache of my undoing.

That day didn't end with a clean slate. But it began with a holy step. And I'll never forget the moment I realized: I can do hard things when I don't do them alone.

I wasn't sure if I was brave or just broken beyond repair. But I remember whispering, 'God, walk with me.' That day, I didn't see flames—but I felt them. The sting of shame. The heat of judgment. The sear of old fears. And yet, I walked out still standing.

There is something undeniably holy about a woman who has walked through fire and still speaks with grace. A woman who survived the unthinkable, and instead of closing her heart, opens her hands. A woman who doesn't just rise from the ashes but carries others out with her.

That woman? She is becoming the breakthrough.

Not because she never broke—but because she did. And when she did, she met a God who refused to let her be shattered without purpose.

In the Bible, fire is not just destruction—it is refinement. For a holy woman, walking through fire does not end in ashes. It ends in glory. Scripture tells us that God walks with us in the fire, not just on the other side of it. The fire becomes a forge for purpose, not a sentence of ruin. Shadrach, Meshach, and Abednego walked through literal flames and came out unsinged. That's not a fairytale—that's a foreshadowing. A promise. A glimpse of how God honors faith in the furnace.

Fire in the Bible isn't just about trial—it's about transformation. Moses was called by God through fire that did not consume. Elijah called down fire to prove God's power. At Pentecost, tongues of fire descended, and the early church was born.

In each case, fire marked the beginning of purpose. Not the end. Not destruction—but divine direction. So, if you've felt the flames, maybe it's not because you're being punished. Maybe it's because you're being positioned.

Fire may have touched your life. Abuse, loss, betrayal—they scorched your soil. But what God plants can still grow. The fire didn't end you. It revealed you. And now, you are becoming the breakthrough not just in theory, but in testimony.

And still—the ashes remain. The dreams that died. The innocence taken. The parts of your past you thought you'd never talk about. But even ashes can speak.

Isaiah 61:3 says He will give "beauty for ashes." That doesn't mean He erases what happened—it means He transforms it. The burned ground becomes holy ground. What you thought was the end becomes the soil where purpose is planted.

Let your ashes breathe. Let them tell the truth. Because God doesn't waste even the smoke.

This chapter is for the woman who has wondered if her story matters. For the one who has questioned if she is allowed to speak. For the one who thinks testimony only belongs to the pulpit, or to the polished.

No. This story belongs to you. Right now. Even in process. Even in progress. Even with the scars still fresh.

When I began to write this book, I didn't start with confidence. I started with trembling fingers and a cracked-open heart. I wrote from the mess, not the mountaintop. I wrote while I was still healing—not after I had it all figured out.

And yet, every time I hit publish, every time I told a piece of the truth I once hid, something broke open in someone else.

They messaged me: "That's my story too."

"I thought I was alone."

"You said what I haven't been able to say."

And that's when I realized: our healing is not just for us. It's for the women still stuck. The ones still silenced. The ones still surviving.

Your healing becomes their hope.

Your voice becomes their permission.

Your breakthrough becomes their blueprint.

I remember a woman who read one of my posts and messaged me privately. "I thought I was the only one," she said. "You wrote what I've never been able to say out loud."

Months later, she sent another message. "I left," she wrote. "I found a safe place. I started over. I'm telling my story now, too."

She didn't have a platform. She didn't have a book deal. She had a voice and a victory. And that was enough.

That's how breakthrough multiplies. One voice. One story. One sacred echo that says, "You're not alone."

When you speak, you light a torch. You say, "I made it out. And so can you."

And each torch lights another. Imagine a line of women, stretched across a battlefield of trauma and truth. One by one, they raise their flames—not to destroy, but to declare. "I was there. And I made it out."

Your torch matters. Even if it flickers. Even if it's small. Someone is walking in the dark behind you, and your flame becomes their first glimpse of hope.

Testimony is not reserved for church stages or viral videos.

Testimony is sacred because it is real.

Your story, your voice, your truth—they are all part of how God reveals His goodness in a broken world. He doesn't just use scripture. He uses you.

He uses your survival as sacred evidence. He uses your tears to water another woman's garden. He uses your scars as signposts toward safety. Just like Esther was used to save her people, just like Ruth was used to carry legacy forward, just like Miriam led with tambourine in hand after the Red Sea split—you are being used.

You are not just a survivor. You are a storyteller.

And storytelling is holy.

When Jesus healed people in the New Testament, they didn't just return to their lives in silence. They told everyone what He did. And their stories changed things.

So will yours.

Being a vessel doesn't mean being perfect. It means being willing.

A vessel holds and pours. And that's what your life does now. You hold the lessons, the tears, the wrestlings, and the wisdom—and you pour them out in kindness. In truth. In testimony.

You might be thinking, Who am I to help anyone else? But friend, you are the exact person.

Because you know what it feels like to lay on the bathroom floor and whisper, God, I can't do this anymore. You know what it feels like to show up to work with swollen eyes and a fake smile. You know what it feels like to parent through pain, to laugh through trauma, to start over when the world felt like it ended.

That makes you qualified. That makes you holy ground.

Your testimony doesn't require perfection. It requires permission— permission from you, to yourself, to be seen and known.

Think of Esther, who risked everything for her people. She didn't feel ready. But she stepped up anyway. Her breakthrough didn't look like bravery at first—it looked like obedience in the middle of fear.

Or Hagar, who ran into the wilderness, only to be met by a God who saw her. She named Him "El Roi"—the God who sees. That was her breakthrough. Not rescue first but being seen.

These women weren't perfect. They were present. And God used their stories to set others free.

You don't need to tell the whole story at once. Sometimes, one truth is enough to change a life.

Your story will:

- Break chains for women still trapped in silence.
- Invite others into healing.
- Show the world that redemption is real.
- Prove that God still moves in everyday lives.

You don't have to write a book. Maybe you tell a friend. Maybe you start a support group. Maybe you share your story in small pieces, in car rides, in coffee shops, on social media, in whispered prayers.

Every offering matters.

You don't have to do something big. Just something.

Maybe you write a letter and never send it. Maybe you start a podcast or whisper your story to a friend over coffee. Maybe you volunteer at a shelter.

Every time you offer your story, you multiply the miracle. You make healing a harvest. You show someone else that resurrection isn't just for Jesus—it's for her too.

Because someone is still sitting in what you survived.

And your truth is their lifeline.

You were never just what happened to you. You were always someone becoming.

When I started this journey, I didn't know who I was. Abuse had clouded my reflection. Survival had muted my voice. But step by step, with God, I started reclaiming what had been stolen:

- My joy.
- My sleep.

- My voice.
- My dreams.
- My presence.

And now, writing these words to you, I realize this is the testimony.

I am still here. And that is holy.

So are you.

Let this be your moment to say, "I am no longer a victim. I am a vessel."

Let this be your declaration: "My story matters. My voice matters. My purpose matters."

You are becoming the breakthrough.

Not just for you. But for every woman who needs a reminder that healing is possible.

Every word you write. Every tear you shed. Every truth you share.

It all becomes a light.

Live It Out Challenge | Tell One True Thing

This week, tell one true thing about your story.

- Write it in your journal.
- Speak it to a safe friend.
- Post it with intention.

Name one part of your journey you've healed from, and declare it out loud:

- "This happened, and I am healing."
- "This broke me, but it did not define me."
- "God is using even this."

Let that truth echo.

Because your voice is powerful.

Your healing is holy.

And your story is someone else's breakthrough.

Anchor Prayer | Here I Am, Lord

God,

Thank You for redeeming every part of my story.

For turning what tried to break me into what now builds others.

Use my voice. Use my pain. Use my healing.

Make me a vessel of truth, of hope, of courage.

Let my story be a testimony that You still set captives free.

Let every word I share become a seed of healing in someone else.

I am no longer ashamed.

I am no longer silent.

I am no longer bound.

I am Yours.

I am ready.

Here I am.

Use me.

Amen.

Brave Enough to Begin Again

"Forget the former things; do not dwell on the past. See, I am doing a new thing! Now it springs up; do you not perceive it? I am making a way in the wilderness and streams in the wasteland." —Isaiah 43:18–19

There comes a quiet but holy moment in healing when grief loosens its grip, and your soul begins to whisper again. It doesn't shout. It doesn't demand. It simply stirs. And the whisper says: It's time. Not because the pain is gone. Not because the scars have vanished. But because somewhere in the depths of your spirit, the ache begins to lean forward. Not toward certainty, but toward possibility. Toward new life. Toward trust.

And still, as that stirring begins, fear is almost always the first voice to respond. It clings to logic, calculation, and self-protection. It offers worst-case scenarios like candy and convinces you that staying stuck is safer than stepping forward. You'll hear it say:

- What if I'm too late?

- What if I'm not healed enough?

- What if they hurt me again?

- What if no one sees me?

- What if I mess this up?

But the voice of faith is different. It's softer, deeper. It doesn't shout over fear—it simply answers it. And when fear says what if, faith replies with even if.

- Even if I'm starting late, God redeems time.

- Even if I'm still healing, He walks with me in process.

- Even if I'm wounded again, He will restore.

- Even if I'm unseen by others, I am known by God.

- Even if I stumble, I will rise because I am upheld.

"Though he may stumble, he will not fall, for the Lord upholds him with his hand."
—Psalm 37:24

Faith doesn't silence fear. It simply makes the decision to move anyway.

Ruth's life had crumbled. Her husband was gone, her homeland behind her, and her future uncertain. She could have stayed in Moab, surrounded by the comfort of familiarity. But she chose to follow Naomi—into Bethlehem, into unknown fields, into a future written only by faith. She didn't know Boaz was waiting. She didn't know she would become the great-grandmother of a king. She just knew that staying stuck in grief wouldn't resurrect her purpose.

Fear whispered, what if you have nothing left?

Faith answered, even if I have nothing, I have God.

Ruth's decision didn't feel glamorous. It looked like gathering scraps from the ground and waking up with aching feet. But her obedience was the soil for redemption. Her courage wasn't loud—it was lived. And that is often how new beginnings come: not in spotlight moments, but in small, consistent acts of hope.

When Jesus died, Mary Magdalene could have disappeared. The story, it seemed, had ended. But she returned to the tomb anyway—faithful in her grief, seeking her Savior even in death. It was there, in the garden, that Jesus met her. She became the first witness of the resurrection, the first voice of the Gospel's most powerful truth: He is risen.

She didn't know how the story would unfold.

But she showed up anyway.

Sometimes healing looks like seeking when you don't yet see.

Sometimes the beginning of new life looks like weeping in a garden and hearing your name spoken by the One who never left you.

When the Israelites returned from exile, they didn't find a temple—they found rubble. And yet, they began to build. Some wept. Some worshiped. Some did both at once. And God received it all.

You may be standing in the ruins of a dream, a relationship, a version of yourself you thought would last. But God is a builder who specializes in broken things. He doesn't wait for the dust to settle. He calls you to begin right where you are.

"Do not despise these small beginnings, for the Lord rejoices to see the work begin." —Zechariah 4:10

Maybe beginning again for you means walking into a room that reminds you of pain—but choosing to walk in anyway. Maybe it's journaling one page, even though the pen feels heavy. Maybe it's applying for something, opening your Bible, trusting someone, or letting go. These beginnings might seem small. But in God's hands, they are sacred.

There is a lie that steals courage before it takes root: You should be further along by now. It sounds practical. It sounds responsible. But it is laced with shame. And God never uses shame as motivation.

He is not disappointed by your pace. He's not comparing your timeline to anyone else's. He knows what you've walked through. He knows what it took for you to get back up. He doesn't rush you—He restores you.

"There is a time for everything, and a season for every activity under the heavens." —Ecclesiastes 3:1

God doesn't operate on our deadlines. He operates in divine timing. You are not behind. You are becoming.

Faith rarely looks like certainty. It looks like shaky hands taking a step. It looks like trying again, even after failure. It looks like hope rising in the most unexpected places.

Faith shows up. It shows up in cracked voices and honest prayers. It shows up in staying when it would be easier to leave and leaving when it would be easier to stay. Faith isn't about knowing how everything turns out. It's about knowing Who walks with you through it.

"Trust in the Lord with all your heart and lean not on your own understanding; in all your ways submit to Him, and He will make your paths straight." —Proverbs 3:5–6

God never asks you to have it all figured out. He simply asks for your yes. That's how the story shifts. That's how resurrection begins.

Live It Out Challenge | Say the Yes

God doesn't wait until we feel strong to stir something new—He speaks into our weakness and still calls us forward. Saying yes doesn't mean you have it all together. It means you trust the One who holds it all together.

Your small step may not seem significant to others, but in heaven's eyes, it's a declaration: I believe God is not done with me.

Reflect in your Heart Notes about what is God inviting you to begin again?

- Name it.
- Write it down.
- Pray over it.
- Then take one small step this week—any step.

Every step you take in faith is not just progress; it's worship.

Declare over your life:

"Even if I don't feel ready, I say yes. I am not too late. I am right on time."

Anchor Prayer | Courage to Begin Again

God,

Thank You for never being finished with me.

Thank You for calling me into new beginnings—

even when I feel afraid.

You are not intimidated by my fears, and

You are not disappointed by my timeline.

Give me the courage to say yes, even if I don't feel ready.

Remind me that You are already in the next step.

Teach me to trust You more than I trust my fear.

Let faith rise within me—

not because everything is certain,

but because You are with me.

Amen.

Joy That Stays

"The joy of the Lord is your strength." – Nehemiah 8:10

There's something deeply sacred about joy that chooses to stay—even when life doesn't get easier.

This chapter is not about the mountaintop moment when everything finally falls into place. It's not about a resolution or a reward. This chapter is about the gritty, defiant, sacred kind of joy that clings to the soul when the bills pile up, when relationships remain complicated, when the grief still lingers, when the anxiety hums quietly in the background. Joy that stays is joy that has roots. And roots don't grow on mountaintops. They grow in the valleys.

For a long time, I confused joy with happiness. I thought joy was the bubbly kind of cheerfulness you see in highlight reels and popular quotes. I believed that to be joyful meant to always smile, to avoid the hard things, or to wear a mask of optimism. But God began to teach me something different.

I learned that joy isn't a feeling you manufacture. It's a fruit you cultivate. It doesn't disappear when the storm rolls in—it anchors you through it. And in the wreckage of my own brokenness, I began to ask God for joy that would stay.

Happiness is circumstantial. It's that rush of dopamine when something goes right: a kind word, a warm meal, a burst of laughter. There's nothing wrong with happiness—in fact, we need it. But happiness is fickle. It ebbs and flows with our environment.

Joy, however, is different. Joy is spiritual. It's not something you feel; it's something you carry.

Where happiness responds to life, joy reframes life. Where happiness waits for things to be good, joy remembers that God is good, even when life isn't.

Happiness is like sunshine—beautiful, welcome, but dependent on the weather. Joy is like an internal fire that doesn't go out, even when the nights are long and cold.

I remember sitting in my car in a grocery store parking lot years ago. I had just enough money to buy what we needed. My bank account was nearly empty, my heart was completely broken, and I was weary. And yet, in that moment, I felt a strange, unexpected peace. A memory surfaced of God's faithfulness during another hard season, and I whispered, "Thank You." I was still grieving. Still exhausted. But I was grateful. That was joy.

That was when I knew the difference. That joy—deep, quiet, holy—wasn't based on what I had. It was based on Who I knew.

Nehemiah 8:10 says, "The joy of the Lord is your strength." Not your achievements. Not your relationships. Not even your own mindset. God's joy—God's delight, God's love, God's unwavering goodness—is what strengthens you.

When the Israelites heard the law for the first time after exile, they wept. Their hearts were broken. But Nehemiah told them not to mourn. Instead, he told them to celebrate, to feast, to rejoice. Why? Because joy was their strength—not shame. Not sorrow. Joy.

The enemy of your soul doesn't fear your happiness. He fears your joy. Because joy makes you unshakable.

Joy says, "Even here, I am loved."

Joy says, "Even now, I will worship."

Joy says, "Even if the situation doesn't change, God is still good—and so I will praise Him."

Joy is the war cry of the woman who walks through loss and still lifts her hands. It is the anthem of the survivor who dares to dance again. It is the song of the healed who remember the pit—and choose joy anyway.

When you reframe joy not as a byproduct of life but as a strength for life, everything changes.

If joy is strength, how do we strengthen it?

We practice it. Just like muscles are built with small, daily repetitions, joy grows through intentional habits.

Here are five daily joy practices that helped me reclaim the joy that stays:

1. Reclaim God's Goodness

Every day, name one way you've seen God's goodness—even if it's small. Did the sun break through your window just right? Did a friend send you an unexpected message? Did your child laugh?

These moments are not accidents. They are evidence.

Joy returns when we choose to see God not as absent, but as present. As active. As good.

Scripture says, "Surely goodness and mercy will follow me all the days of my life." (Psalm 23:6) But we must train our eyes to see it. Write it down. Speak it aloud.

2. Experience His Presence

Joy isn't something you earn. It's something you experience with God. Psalm 16:11 reminds us: "In Your presence is fullness of joy."

So much of my healing happened not because the pain disappeared, but because I chose to sit with God in it. Some days I simply whispered, "I'm here, Lord." Other days, I cried on the floor in silence. But every moment invited His presence. And every moment with Him gave me joy.

You don't need a perfect prayer to experience His presence. Just come as you are. That's where joy grows.

3. Rejoice in God's Love

We rejoice not because life is perfect, but because love is. God's love does not waver based on our performance or pain. It remains.

Romans 8:38–39 declares that nothing—not death, not fear, not trauma, not failure—can separate us from the love of God in Christ Jesus.

Joy that stays is joy that abides in this truth. It's not a feeling; it's a deep-rooted confidence that we are loved beyond measure.

Make it a daily rhythm to rejoice in that. Say it out loud. Write it on your mirror. Whisper it over your heart. "I am deeply loved by God today."

4. Be Thankful in Prayer

Gratitude and joy are deeply connected.

Philippians 4:6–7 instructs us to present our requests to God with thanksgiving. And what happens? "The peace of God, which surpasses all understanding, will guard your hearts and minds."

Every night, I began to end my day by naming three things I was thankful for. Some days it was hard. Some days it felt like scraping the bottom of an empty barrel. But even then, I found something: I'm breathing. I'm healing. I'm trying.

Gratitude trains the soul to expect goodness again.

5. Find Joy in the Smallest of Moments

Joy isn't always loud. Sometimes it's a soft smile. A long exhale. The smell of fresh laundry. A perfectly steeped cup of tea. A sunrise.

When you slow down enough to notice the beauty that already surrounds you, you begin to realize joy was never gone. You just weren't looking for it.

Keep a record of these small moments. They become the testimony of your strength.

Some people may look at your joy and think you're naïve.

They don't know what it cost you to smile again. To hope again. To laugh without guilt. To breathe without fear. To dream beyond survival. But friend, let me say this: joy is not weakness. It is bravery in its purest form.

It's easy to numb. Easy to avoid. Easy to stay cynical.

It's hard to rejoice on purpose.

Joy is the bold declaration that the enemy did not win. It is the daily refusal to let bitterness root deeper than beauty. It is the act of holding both sorrow and celebration in the same breath—and choosing to sing anyway.

If joy still feels foreign to you, that's okay.

Sometimes, trauma silences our ability to experience joy. It's not that it's gone—it's just buried. Covered in grief. Layered in fear.

But joy will come back. And you don't have to force it. You just have to make space for it.

Start small. Write yourself a note. Take a walk. Listen to a worship song. Laugh at a meme. Call a friend. Let yourself notice one good thing.

Then another. And another.

Joy is like sunlight after winter. You'll squint at first. It might feel uncomfortable. But let it warm you again.

You may still be healing. You may still be rebuilding. You may still be unsure.

But joy is not waiting for your life to be perfect.

It is waiting for you to notice.

It is hiding in the ordinary. Nestled into sacred moments. Grown through gratitude. Watered in worship. Anchored in God's presence.

Joy is not a reward for the healed—it's a companion for the healing.

And it stays. Even in the mess. Even in the questions. Even in the wilderness.

Joy stays because Jesus does.

So, laugh again. Smile again. Sing again. Dance in your kitchen. Cry while grateful. Pray while tired. Rest in His love.

You are not weak for needing joy. You are strong for seeking it.

And I promise you this:

Joy that comes from the Lord will stay.

Even here. Especially here.

Live It Out Challenge | The Joy Journal

You are invited to practice joy—not because life is perfect, but because God is present.

Here's your challenge:

For the next 7 days, keep a running list of small joys in your Heart Notes. It can be one joy a day or a handful. Use your notes app, a journal, or sticky notes—whatever works for you. These joys can be anything:

- A warm drink

- A hug

- A moment of clarity

- A verse that speaks to you

- A quiet moment of peace

- A child's giggle

- A prayer whispered with hope

At the end of the week, set aside a quiet moment.

Read them out loud.

Let those small joys echo back into your soul. Let them remind you that joy is still here. Let them strengthen you.

Then, speak this over yourself:

"The joy of the Lord is my strength." —Nehemiah 8:10

Anchor Prayer | A Prayer for Joy That Stays

God, my source of joy—

Sometimes life feels heavy, and joy feels far away.

But You remind me that joy doesn't come from perfect days—

it comes from knowing You are with me.

Help me notice the good things, even the small ones.

Help me smile again, laugh again, breathe deep, and feel peace.

Even when things are still hard, show me that joy is still possible.

You are my strength.

You are my steady place.

Thank You for joy that doesn't fade, even when life changes.

Grow that joy in me every day.

Today I choose joy—because I choose You.

Amen.

The Ministry of Ordinary Days

"So whether you eat or drink or whatever you do, do it all for the glory of God."— 1 Corinthians 10:31

What If Ordinary Was Holy? We live in a culture that worships the extraordinary.

We're trained to chase big dreams, loud platforms, highlight reels, and the hustle of "doing more." We equate purpose with productivity. Ministry with microphones. Holiness with high places.

But God?

God often whispers through the ordinary.

From Genesis to Revelation, the Bible paints a picture very different from our modern mindset. God doesn't just show up in burning bushes and parted seas. He shows up in fields and tents, in kitchens and boats, in prisons and caves, and—most often—in people doing very ordinary things.

The ministry of ordinary days is not about making our lives flashy or famous. It's about living in such a way that we don't miss the divine that is already woven into our dust.

Biblical "ordinary" isn't ordinary at all. In fact, God makes ordinary things holy:

- Moses was tending sheep when he saw the burning bush.

- David was delivering lunch to his brothers when he stumbled into Goliath's battlefield.

- Ruth was gathering leftovers in a field when her future changed forever.

- Mary was folding laundry in Nazareth when Gabriel interrupted her plans with a divine assignment.

- Jesus spent most of His life as a carpenter—God in flesh, working with splinters and nails long before the cross.

The pattern is clear: God chooses ordinary as His launching pad for glory.

He doesn't wait for the perfect setting or a spotlight. He enters the quiet. He dwells in the everyday. He performs miracles in kitchens, not just on mountaintops.

The modern world trains us to dismiss ordinary.

Ordinary is seen as boring, forgettable, or not enough. We're told to "do something big," "make a name," or "be remarkable." As a result, we rush through daily tasks like they're obstacles to real life instead of opportunities to be present in it.

We multitask through meals, scroll through conversations, and resent the quiet. We wonder if folding laundry matters. We wonder if grocery shopping with a toddler counts for anything. We wonder if we're wasting our life when we're not "changing the world."

But maybe the real change happens in the places we least expect.

Maybe ordinary isn't something to escape.

Maybe it's something to enter into fully—with open eyes and holy expectation.

I remember one particular morning, years into my healing journey, standing barefoot in front of the kitchen sink. Dishes were piled high, the boys were bantering in the background, and my to-do list was growing longer by the second.

It felt like a small kind of suffocation.

The kind that says, "This can't be ministry. This can't be purpose. This is just...survival."

And yet, in that moment, I felt the whisper of God break through the noise:

"This is where I meet you too."

Not in the stage or the breakthrough or the perfectly crafted prayer.

Right here. In the dishwater. In the socks on the floor. In the repetition.

It wasn't glamorous. But it was holy.

I realized then that the sacred isn't reserved for Sunday mornings. It's buried in the mundane, waiting for us to notice.

We often separate our spiritual lives from our daily lives.

But in God's Kingdom, everything counts.

Make a bed with love is holy.

Packing a lunch with prayer is ministry.

Texting a friend encouragement, making a pot of coffee, showing up for a sibling, wiping down the counters—it's all sacred ground when you do it with intention and love.

You are living a ministry life, even when no one sees it. Maybe especially then.

Jesus said in Matthew 6:4, "Your Father, who sees what is done in secret, will reward you."

He sees you when you show up in small ways.

He sees you loving people who are hard to love.

He sees your faithfulness in quiet corners.

You don't need a pulpit to preach.

Your actions are already telling a story of grace.

The truth is: God doesn't need you to do more. He simply invites you to be present with Him where you already are.

That's the invitation of ordinary days: to notice the holy happening right now.

Try this for a moment.

- The next time you do laundry, say a prayer over the person who wears each item.

- When you make a meal, thank God for the hands that grew the food and the ones who will eat it.

- When you drive your kids to school or yourself to work, turn off the noise and whisper, "God, be here too."

- When you're standing in line at the grocery store, look at the people around you. Notice them. Pray for them.

These aren't wasted minutes. They are windows for wonder.

You don't need to strive to be extraordinary. You need to be awake in the ordinary.

Intention is about choosing to live on purpose, even in the smallest acts.

Colossians 3:23 reminds us, "Whatever you do, work at it with all your heart, as working for the Lord."

That means vacuuming counts.

That means email replies count.

That means choosing joy on a Tuesday afternoon is an act of worship.

Living with intention doesn't mean adding more to your plate. It means looking at your plate and asking, "Where is God already in this?"

It means slowing down long enough to hear the sacred hum in the background of your day.

It means living like your ordinary rhythms are part of God's masterpiece—and they are.

There's a strange kind of healing that happens in routine.

When you've lived through trauma or chaos, normalcy can feel unfamiliar—maybe even boring. But slowly, it becomes a balm. A rhythm. A place where your nervous system can breathe again.

Ordinary days don't mean nothing is happening.

They mean healing is happening at a pace your soul can handle.

Sometimes, the repetition is the redemption. You show up. You love again. You cook again. You try again.

Each act says, "I'm still here. I'm still becoming."

And God is with you in every step of it.

Love Big Challenge | Ordinary Acts of Love

You are not missing your calling because you are folding towels. You are not wasting your life because you're standing in a drop-off line. You are not behind because your ministry looks like showing up faithfully in places the world ignores.

This week, choose one ordinary action to turn into an extraordinary act of love.

- Fold someone's laundry and leave a kind note in their drawer.

- Pack a lunch with a prayer tucked inside.

- Offer a smile and kind word to the barista or cashier.

- Send a text to someone who might feel unseen.

- Light a candle and pray for your home while sweeping the floor.

Love doesn't have to be loud.

In God's economy, the small is sacred.

Love big by showing up with your whole heart—even in the littlest things.

Anchor Prayer | Meet Me in the Everyday

God of the Ordinary,

Sometimes I think I need to do something big to matter.

But You remind me that You meet me in the ordinary—

in the middle of the dishes, the meetings,

the pickups, the piles of laundry.

You are not waiting for me to be impressive.

You are just waiting for me to be present.

So here I am, Lord.

Open my eyes to the sacred that surrounds me.

Remind me that every act of love counts.

Let my routines become worship.

Let my chores become prayer.

Let my small choices make room for big grace.

I don't need to be famous—I want to be faithful.

Help me live this ordinary life with extraordinary love.

And let me never forget: You are here, too.

Amen.

20

Living Big. Loving Bigger.

"Now to him who is able to do immeasurably more than all we ask or imagine, according to his power that is at work within us." —Ephesians 3:20

There is a moment in every healing journey when the past no longer defines you, and the future doesn't scare you.

A sacred shift occurs—a moment when you realize you are not simply a survivor of your story, but the author of what comes next. That moment is not marked by fanfare or flashes of glory. Sometimes, it's as quiet as exhaling without apology. Sometimes, it's as simple as laughter returning to your voice or peace to your chest. That moment, dear reader, is now.

This chapter is not just a conclusion—it's a commissioning.

A release.

A holy reminder that everything you've walked through has been leading you here.

The pain, the silence, the long nights you never thought would end—none of it was wasted. This is where healing becomes legacy. Where trauma transforms into testimony. Where the shadows of what you endured no longer have permission to dim the light of who you're becoming. Living big and loving bigger isn't a motto. It's a manifesto. It's how we reclaim our lives, one brave breath at a time.

It's how we stop performing for love and start becoming it. It's how we rise from ashes with joy in our bones and fire in our belly. It's how we go from silenced to sacred.

When I look back at the woman I used to be, I no longer just see sadness or shame. I see sacred survival. I see a woman who crawled out of fear and stood anyway. I see a mother who made peanut butter and jelly sandwiches for her kids while silently falling apart in the bathroom. I see a leader who whispered, "Use me, God," even while questioning her worth. And then I look at who I am today, and I hardly recognize her—in the best way. I see the woman who laughs from her belly, who leads with boldness and compassion. The one who tells the truth even when it trembles and writes stories that heal. The woman who prays in parking lots and walks into rooms with scripture on her tongue.

That woman is me. And if it can be me, it can absolutely be you.

Living big isn't about accumulating status or striving for worldly success. It's about waking up and saying yes to the fullness of who God made you to be.

It means walking into rooms where you once felt small and choosing not to shrink. It's using your voice, not with arrogance, but with holy authority. It's taking up space—not out of entitlement but out of reverence for the God who created you on purpose and for a purpose. It's saying yes to the things that scare you because they also stretch you. Living big means refusing to settle for survival when sacred abundance is being offered by the hands of a God who sees you and calls you by name. Here's what it might look like when you start to live big:

1. You take the mic—even when your voice shakes—and share the truth of what you've walked through.

2. You walk in joy, not because life is easy, but because your soul is no longer hostage to fear.

3. You stand tall in rooms where you once felt invisible, because you know now that you belong.

The first time I stood behind a podium and spoke publicly about what I had survived, I was shaking. I wasn't sure I'd make it through the story without falling apart. But by the end, three women stood in front of me with tears in their eyes and said, "That was my story too." That's what living big does—it unlocks other people's freedom. It opens the door not just for ourselves, but for every woman who's still trapped in the silence we once knew.

There is a new door on the soul house I've been rebuilding all these chapters. This one has my name carved into it. And I no longer knock. I walk in. I belong in this life. And so do you.

For those of us who have spent years learning how to survive, it's often hard to recognize the difference between survival and freedom. So let me offer a glimpse. Before healing, I hid in bathroom stalls to cry. After healing, I prayed out loud in courthouse hallways. Before, I shrunk in silence. After, I sang in the car with the windows down. Before, I apologized for having needs. After, I advocated for boundaries that honored my worth.

That's the fruit of living big.

That's the transformation that happens when God rewrites the narrative and you stop rehearsing who you were and start rising into who you are. Now let's talk about love. Because if living big is about reclaiming identity, loving bigger is about how we live it out in the world. Loving bigger means loving with more courage, more compassion, and more boundaries. Yes—boundaries. Real love, the kind that heals and holds, doesn't smother or shrink. It expands. It protects peace without closing doors. It lets go without losing heart.

Here are three ways to love bigger without losing yourself:

1. "I love you, and I need space to heal right now."

2. "I can't carry that for you, but I will sit beside you."

3. "I am not responsible for how others receive my healing."

To love bigger is to show up for yourself in the mirror each morning and speak kindness instead of criticism. It's to say, "I forgive you," to the version of you that only knew how to survive. It's calling a friend just to say, "You're not alone." It's saying yes to your children when they ask to play—even when you're tired—because you've learned that presence is more powerful than perfection. It's praying for the woman you used to be and for the one you're still becoming.

Here's what loving bigger often looks like in practice:

- Choosing silence over retaliation.

- Pausing instead of people-pleasing.

- Saying yes to joy even when grief lingers.

Loving bigger is a decision. It's made every day in the quiet corners of our lives. And here's the ripple effect: every time you love bigger, you plant a seed in someone else. Your children learn what safety feels like. Your friends feel freer in your presence. Your colleagues are drawn to the peace you now carry. You will not just change your life. You'll change your legacy.

Legacy isn't what we leave behind when we die. It's what we build into others while we're still here. It's the cup of coffee offered in silence. The note tucked into a child's lunchbox. The listening ear that says, "I've been there, and I see you." It's how you show up with healing, again and again.

Let me offer a lens to view that legacy through. Ask yourself:

Who am I healing for?

Where can my healing plant seeds?

What do I want people to feel when they're around me?

These aren't rhetorical questions. They are the blueprint for living big and loving bigger. Because your life is not meant to be a monument to your pain, but a lighthouse for others still finding their way through the fog.

Live Big Challenge | Your Brave Woman Declaration

Now, I want to challenge you.

Write your Brave Woman Declaration—one paragraph. One truth. One moment of power about who you are now and what you are claiming in your Heart Notes. Say it out loud. Save it. Write it on your mirror. Post it on your phone. Let it be a daily anchor for the days when you feel unsteady.

Then choose one bold act of healing this month. Just one.

- Call the friend.

- Sign up for the dream.

- Say no when you usually say yes.

Finally, name one woman you want to walk beside this year. Your story might be her survival guide.

Because it matters.

Because you matter.

Because your life is a testimony.

Anchor Prayer | My Life, Reclaimed

God,

Thank You for being the God of full circles.

For writing redemption into every chapter.

I give You my story, my strength, and my surrender.

Help me to live big—boldly, fully, freely.

Teach me to love bigger—with courage,

with clarity, and with compassion.

Let my life be a light, my words be a balm,

and my home be a haven.

I release what was.

I reclaim what is.

I rejoice in what's to come.

Let it be legacy.

Let it be love.

Amen.

Heart Notes

This is the part of the story where I step back—and you step forward. You've walked with me through ashes and rebuilding, through silent nights and sacred awakenings, through pain that once named me and a love that redefined me. We've named trauma. We've told the truth. We've stood in front of mirrors and declared healing. And now, here at the close of these pages, I want to leave you with something more than a conclusion. I want to leave you with a sacred space—your space. This chapter belongs to you.

These heart notes are an invitation to linger. To reflect. To let what you've read settle into the soil of your own story. They are a quiet corner where your tears are welcome, your laughter is holy, and your voice is safe. This is your altar, your journal, your sanctuary. No performance. No pressure. Just presence.

As I reclaimed my life one courageous moment at a time, I found that the real transformation wasn't in the loud declarations or the mountaintop moments. It happened in the in-between—in the quiet, the unseen, the minutes where I chose truth over denial, joy over numbness, and hope over fear. It happened every time I decided that who God said I was mattered more than what anyone else had done to me.

If there's one truth, I pray you carry from these pages, it's this: you are not too broken, too late, or too far gone to be made whole. The same God who met me on the floor of my pain will meet you in yours. The same Spirit who gave me breath when I didn't want to keep breathing will breathe fresh life into your soul. The same love that pulled me out of hiding is reaching for you, even now.

So here, in this final chapter, I want to offer more than closure. I want to offer tools for continuation. Because healing doesn't end with the last sentence—it begins with the ones you write next.

Reflection Pages

Use these lines as sacred space. Write what hurt. Write what healed. Write what surprised you. Write what set you free. Let these pages carry your honesty like incense—raw, rising, real. There is no wrong way to reflect when you're telling the truth.

- What moment from this book spoke the loudest to your heart?

- What pain have you finally named?

- What brave decision are you ready to make next?

- What does "living big" look like for you today?

Favorite Scriptures to Carry You Forward

These verses were anchors in my storm. May they be lighthouses in yours.

- "The Lord is close to the brokenhearted and saves those who are crushed in spirit." —Psalm 34:18

- "Forget the former things; do not dwell on the past. See, I am doing a new thing!" —Isaiah 43:18–19

- "You intended to harm me, but God intended it for good." — Genesis 50:20

- "There is now no condemnation for those who are in Christ Jesus." —Romans 8:1

- "God is within her, she will not fall." —Psalm 46:5

Add your own. Make it personal. Let scripture become your sword.

Truths to Revisit

Come back to these whenever you forget. These are the declarations that rewrite shame, restore strength, and reclaim peace.

- I am not what happened to me—I am who God is healing in me.

- I do not have to apologize for surviving.

- My voice matters.

- My boundaries are sacred.

- God is not done writing my story.

- I am safe. I am seen. I am still standing.

- I was made for more than just making it.

- Love is still a promise—and I am still worthy of it.

This is not the end. This is the exhale before your next brave inhale.

The pages may be closing, but your legacy is just beginning. Go live it—fully, freely, unapologetically. Go write the rest of your story with the pen of grace and the ink of healing. Go speak life over dry bones and joy into weary places. Go show the world what it looks like to live big and love bigger—not just once, but every single day.

You are no longer who you were.

You are no longer only what you survived.

You are living proof that redemption is real.

That beauty can rise from ashes.

That love can find you again.

That faith still speaks in wilderness places.

This chapter isn't closure.

It's a commissioning.

Now go—

Live big. Love bigger. Leave legacy.

And never, ever forget:

You are the testimony.

My Anchor Prayer for You

Beloved Daughter, Brave Soul—

May you always remember that the God who brought you this far

is not finished with you yet.

May you know, deep in your bones,

that you are not too much, too broken, too late, or too far gone.

You are just in time for grace.

May every scar you carry become a doorway for compassion,

every wound a window for wisdom,

every silence a stage for your voice to rise.

I pray that you will never again

shrink to fit someone else's comfort or

carry what was never yours to hold.

That you will walk away from what tried to break you and

walk toward the One who rebuilds with

beauty, laughter, and light.

May you speak truth without apology.

May you grieve with courage and hope with abandon.

May you dance in your kitchen, pray in your car, and

preach freedom by how you live.

I pray that your healing will become someone else's hallelujah.

That your story will set captives free.

That your life will sing of restoration—loud, fearless, and holy.

And when you forget—because we all do—

may you remember this:

You are loved. You are chosen. You are still becoming.

The past doesn't get the final word.

God does. And His word over you is good.

So go on, beautiful one—Live big. Love bigger.

Leave a legacy of light.

And know, always—You are the testimony.

Amen.

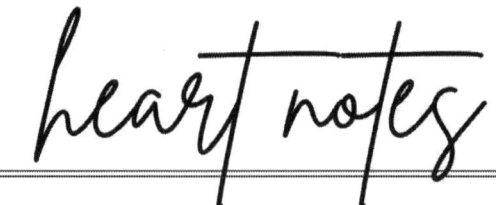

DATE: _____   CHAPTER: _____

_____

_____

_____

_____

_____

_____

_____

_____

_____

_____

_____

_____

_____

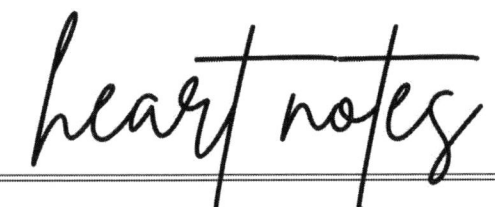

DATE: _____ CHAPTER: _____

_____

_____

_____

_____

_____

_____

_____

_____

_____

_____

_____

_____

_____

_____

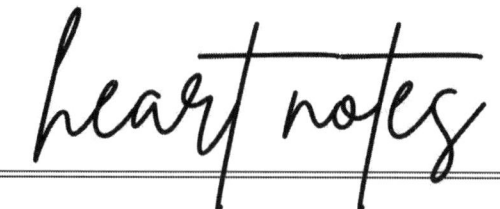

DATE: _____ CHAPTER: _____

DATE: _____ CHAPTER: _____

_____

_____

_____

_____

_____

_____

_____

_____

_____

_____

_____

_____

_____

_____

_____

_____

_____

DATE: _____ CHAPTER: _____

_____

_____

_____

_____

_____

_____

_____

_____

_____

_____

_____

_____

_____

_____

_____

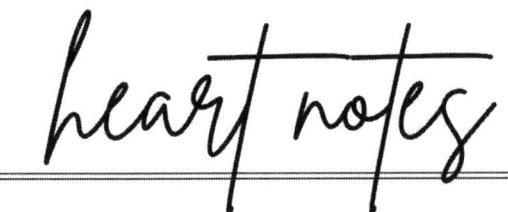

heart notes

DATE: _____ CHAPTER: _____

_____

_____

_____

_____

_____

_____

_____

_____

_____

_____

_____

_____

_____

_____

_____

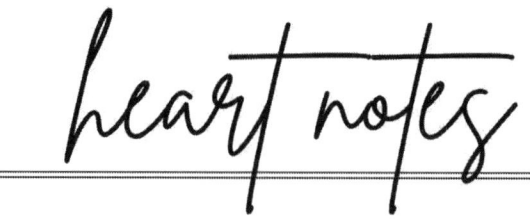

DATE: _____ CHAPTER: _____

_____

_____

_____

_____

_____

_____

_____

_____

_____

_____

_____

_____

_____

_____

_____

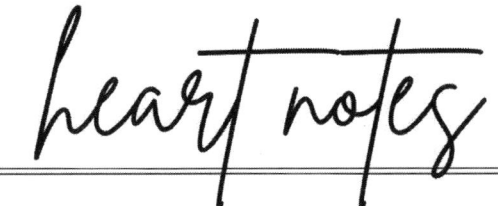

DATE: _____ CHAPTER: _____

_____

_____

_____

_____

_____

_____

_____

_____

_____

_____

_____

_____

_____

_____

_____

DATE: _____ CHAPTER: _____

_____

_____

_____

_____

_____

_____

_____

_____

_____

_____

_____

_____

_____

heart notes

DATE: _____ CHAPTER: _____

_____

_____

_____

_____

_____

_____

_____

_____

_____

_____

_____

_____

_____

_____

_____

_____

_____

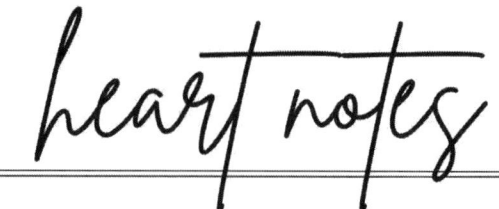

DATE: _____ CHAPTER: _____

_____

_____

_____

_____

_____

_____

_____

_____

_____

_____

_____

_____

_____

_____

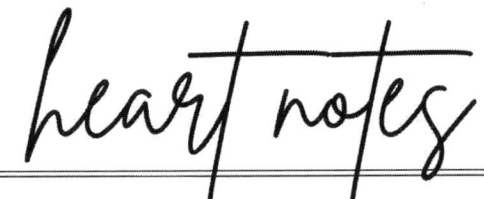

DATE: _____ CHAPTER: _____

_____

_____

_____

_____

_____

_____

_____

_____

_____

_____

_____

_____

_____

DATE: _____ CHAPTER: _____

_____

_____

_____

_____

_____

_____

_____

_____

_____

_____

_____

_____

_____

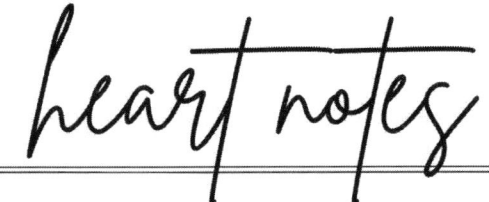

heart notes

DATE: _____ CHAPTER: _____

_____

_____

_____

_____

_____

_____

_____

_____

_____

_____

_____

_____

_____

_____

_____

_____

DATE: _____ CHAPTER: _____

_____

_____

_____

_____

_____

_____

_____

_____

_____

_____

_____

_____

_____

_____

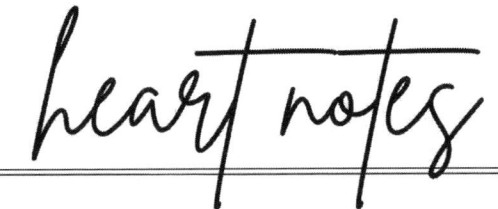

DATE: _____ CHAPTER: _____

_____

_____

_____

_____

_____

_____

_____

_____

_____

_____

_____

_____

_____

_____

_____

_____

_____

_____

DATE: CHAPTER:

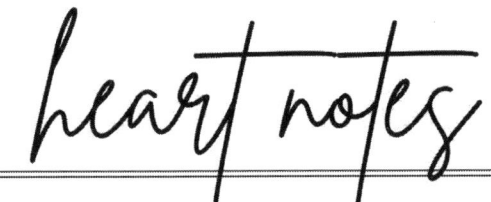

DATE: _____ CHAPTER: _____

_____

_____

_____

_____

_____

_____

_____

_____

_____

_____

_____

_____

_____

_____

_____

_____

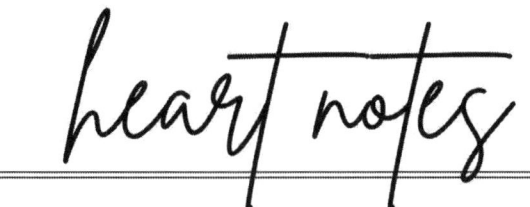

DATE: _____   CHAPTER: _____

_____

_____

_____

_____

_____

_____

_____

_____

_____

_____

_____

_____

_____

_____

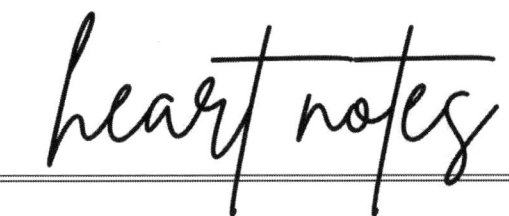

DATE: _____ CHAPTER: _____

_____

_____

_____

_____

_____

_____

_____

_____

_____

_____

_____

_____

_____

_____

DATE: _____ CHAPTER: _____

_____

_____

_____

_____

_____

_____

_____

_____

_____

_____

_____

_____

_____

_____

_____

DATE: _____ CHAPTER: _____

_____

_____

_____

_____

_____

_____

_____

_____

_____

_____

_____

_____

_____

_____

_____

DATE: _____ CHAPTER: _____

_____

_____

_____

_____

_____

_____

_____

_____

_____

_____

_____

_____

_____

_____

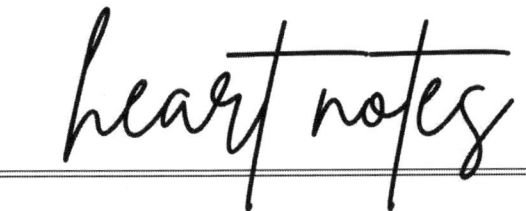

heart notes

DATE: _____   CHAPTER: _____

_____

_____

_____

_____

_____

_____

_____

_____

_____

_____

_____

_____

_____

_____

_____

DATE: _____ CHAPTER: _____

_____

_____

_____

_____

_____

_____

_____

_____

_____

_____

_____

_____

_____

_____

DATE: _____ CHAPTER: _____

_____

_____

_____

_____

_____

_____

_____

_____

_____

_____

_____

_____

_____

Made in the USA
Monee, IL
29 August 2025

23284454R00131